GUIDEPOSTS

ERMA BOMBECK

~ A Life in Humor ~

ERMA BOMBECK

A Life in Humor

Susan Edwards

CARMEL • NEW YORK 10512

This Guideposts edition is published by special arrangement with Avon Books.

Copyright © 1997 by Bill Adler Books, Inc.
Typeset by Composition Technologies, Inc.
ISBN 0-380-97482-7

Library of Congress Cataloging in Publication Data:
Edwards, Susan 1948–
  Erma Bombeck : a life in humor/by Susan Edwards.
    p.   cm.
  1. Bombeck, Erma—Biography. 2. Women authors, American—20th century—Biography. 3. Humorists, American—20th century—Biography. I. Title.
PS3552.059Z65 1997   96–47137
814′.54—dc21   CIP

Printed in the U.S.A.

I am most grateful to Bruce Cassiday for his creative efforts in assisting me in putting the book together.

Contents

ERMA BOMBECK

~ A Life in Humor ~

CHAPTER ONE

A Happy Heart

In a place poetically called "the Valley of the Sun"—a great distance from the place where she was born and later grew to fame as a humorist—Erma Bombeck was eulogized on a beautiful Monday morning in April 1996 by the bishop of Phoenix as "a beam of light and hope...an uplift for the spirit."

Said the Most Reverend Thomas J. O'Brien, "If ever there was a person I wish could come back from the dead, it is Erma. God knows what she would write about that experience. Although I'm not sure if God would like it."

The funeral held at St. Thomas the Apostle

Roman Catholic Church was open to the public—as would be expected for someone of Erma Bombeck's lifestyle and stature. Almost twelve hundred seats were filled, with television trucks lining the parking lot. The list of mourners included celebrities such as talk-show host Phil Donahue, a longtime friend of Erma's, and lifelong friends like Jeanne and Tom Leist of Oakwood, Ohio, along with devoted readers whom the writer had never met, though they called her "friend."

A friend of Erma and her husband Bill since high school, Tom Leist recalled, "She remained just as good a friend after she became famous as she was before."

"Family Circus" cartoonist Bil Keane, who had collaborated with Erma Bombeck on one of her many best-selling books, noted, "She was a sincerely nice friend. She laughed a lot."

Art Buchwald, a longtime friend of Erma's, later said, "She was one of the few columnists who really was unique, and between her books and her column and her public appearances, she brought joy to an awful lot of people. And she was a friend, so I will really miss her."

The Reverend Robert Skagen remembered her as much more than just a columnist who quipped that kids might be considered "punishments from God." "She gave us not only humor and joy, but solid, serious advice on how to love one another and serve one another," he said.

A fellow campaigner for the Equal Rights Amendment, Liz Carpenter remembered her good friend this way: "Everything Erma Bombeck touched turned to life. Her gift of laughter made the daily humdrum chores lighter. We all lost a darling friend and a happy heart."

Raymond L. Fitz, president of the University of Dayton, where Erma and Bill Bombeck earned their college degrees, observed, "Erma taught us to appreciate the vocation of motherhood. [She] helped us to understand the plight of women in our society, and she gave her energies to changing this situation."

Bombeckian one-liners silently echoed throughout the church that day, and everyone was quick to recall a personal favorite:

> *I cook enough spaghetti to feed Sicily and no one shows. I make two small pieces of leftover pizza for dinner and they fly in from out of state.*

I have just come up with a wonderful solution on how to end all wars. Let men give the directions on how to get there.

I think that a man who reads the paper out loud to you, or rips out stories before you get to see it, does not deserve to live.

Never lend your car to anyone to whom you have given birth.

Here was a woman who seemed to laugh at anything that frustrated or annoyed her. Ironically so, since her life held a number of bitter twists. Yet in spite of those tragic turns of fate, she laughed the sorrow from her life.

When she was only nine years old, her father died of a heart attack. Her mother had no family: she had been brought up in an orphanage. Luckily, grandparents on her father's side took them in. Erma, who was used to being the focus of the family, became one of many in a large family. Though the Great Depression was now in full swing, Erma was the only girl in her class whose mother worked for a living. When it came time for college, Erma went to work to earn her way, thereby foregoing the social environment of campus life and becoming something of a loner.

Though her courtship with Bill Bombeck and their eventual marriage had their blissful moments, they, too, were not entirely trouble-free.

Soon after her marriage, Erma found that she was unable to conceive. Because she had decided to quit her job to raise a family, she was in a quandary about what to do with her life. Eventually the Bombecks adopted a girl. Then, a year later, she had a child of her own—a boy—and, later on, another boy.

However, her greatest source of trouble was her health. In her later years she was diagnosed with breast cancer and underwent a modified radical mastectomy. Several years after that, she had a kidney failure and, while waiting for a kidney transplant, began a four-times-a-day at-home dialysis treatment. The transplant was a failure and ultimately caused complications that led to her death.

This is not the story of a lucky woman. And yet no matter what happened, she kept others laughing—and herself, too.

She was an extraordinary woman, a brave woman, and most of those who knew her or just read her column admired the stout heart that kept her going.

Even strangers wrote letters of sympathy at her death.

I've just lost one of my best friends. Over the years we have spent so much time together. Erma is kind of like a therapist to me. She helped me cope through many difficult stages of life. Looking back at when I read each of her books over the last twenty-five years is like a trip down memory lane.

—Dee Ader

I do know that during my most trying times with lupus it was her humor, thoughtful wit, and her way of being able to adjust to life, [that] caused me to have laughter in my life and to remember that I'm not to take myself too seriously, that I not forget the many blessings that are in my life. She will be missed dearly.

—Rachel Estrada

Her work really hit me because I am a very firm advocate of kids not rushing into adulthood, and one of the things she said was, "It's so much better to close the door gently on childhood than to slam it." That really hit home. I always preach to my kids to enjoy [childhood], it won't last too long.

—Gina Gali

After five kids and over two decades of being a mother, I could pretty much identify with most every commentary she'd ever made on the subject. Her humor and her ability to take life's little aggravations and to make me laugh has always buoyed me up in many a stormy sea.

—Janice Havlik

A few years ago I had the pleasure of sitting next to Erma and her husband on a flight...to Phoenix. We had a very pleasant conversation and all laughed a lot. By the end of the flight I felt as though I had made some new friends. While I'm sure they could afford it, they didn't fly first class. They were back in coach with the rest of us common folk. There was no pretension or arrogance. She exuded the dignity of being "common." I miss her weekly reality checks. God bless you, Erma.

—Bruce Litke

One passage I read over and over again [is

in] her book Motherhood, the Second Oldest Profession. *It has a passage for mothers with handicapped children, and I have a handicapped child. I read it over and over again when I'm not feeling good or I'm down. It just makes me feel better.... The passage made me feel like it was written for me.*

—*Jeanne Romansky*

She had a terrific and unique talent that probably won't be seen again in our lifetime. Only she could write about the mysteries of panty hose and let you know you had been there. As she writes her column now for the Heavenly Gazette, *even God himself will have a chuckle.*

—*Beverly Rowles*

I was so profoundly moved by the loss of Erma Bombeck. I think that those of us who are in the over-fifty stage just completely related to her and understood what she was saying. She was so much a part of our lives for so long.

—*Joyce Taylor*

Neil A. Grauer, a Baltimore writer, heard from Erma occasionally following the publication of his

1984 book *Wits & Sages,* which profiled her and eleven other outstanding American newspaper columnists. In the book he dubbed her "The Socrates of the Ironing Board." "She was a courageous performer at the end," he said.

Her fellow humor columnist Dave Barry said, "Erma Bombeck taught those of us who write columns that the funniest things are the things that our readers know the best—houses, cars, kitchens, and of course, kids."

"Just mention her name and I smile," said Andrew Ciofalo, a journalism professor at Loyola College in Baltimore, who read her column regularly when he and his wife were raising their children. "She would see the humor in the everyday occurrences of life that seem so difficult and make them more tolerable. Just as you walk through the day now and have a [Jerry Seinfeld] moment, you would walk through your life having Bombeck moments."

Descriptions of other Bombeck moments might have been drifting about that church in the Valley of the Sun that morning—one-liners bearing the unmistakable mark of Erma's typewriter:

I should have never given birth to more children than we had car windows.

9

A child develops individuality long before he develops taste. I have seen my kid straggle into the kitchen in the morning with outfits that need only one accessory: an empty gin bottle.

If a man watches sixteen consecutive quarters of football, he can be declared legally dead.

The hippopotamus is a vegetarian and looks like a wall. Lions who eat only red meat are sleek and slim. Are nutritionists on the wrong track?

The 1990s did not please Erma Bombeck any more than they pleased the rest of us. Here's a snippet of a Bombeck piece addressing her inability to speak her son's language:

ERMA: So, how are you coming mainstreaming your talents?

SON: There was an ad for a pizza delivery boy, but it wasn't meaningful.

ERMA: Fulfillment without gratification is just the tip of the iceberg.

SON: Boy! Isn't that the truth! Choices. That's what life is all about.

ERMA: Have you tried networking?

SON: Negative. There's no real esteem there,
        you know what I mean?

ERMA: I know exactly. Pressure without upward
        mobility is just another meaningless ex-
        pression of verbal skills.

SON: You really do understand, don't you?

ERMA: I have always said that challenge without
        inadequacy is the social glue that holds
        us all together.

SON: Boy, Mom, I never dreamed you knew
        how I felt. If we had had this dialogue
        ten years ago, maybe we would have had
        a better relationship with one another.
        I'm going to try what you said.

"I'd have given anything," Erma wrote, "to know
what I had *said*."

Erma Bombeck was a versatile writer. Yes, she
was a humorist, always ready to skewer something
with an apropos stiletto of wit. But sometimes she
tackled serious subjects.

"When I was a little kid, a father was like the light
in the refrigerator," she wrote. "Every house had one,
but no one really knew what either of them did once
the door was shut.... Whenever I played house, the

mother doll had a lot to do. I never knew what to do with the daddy doll, so I had him say, 'I'm going off to work now,' and threw him under the bed.

"When I was nine years old, my father didn't get up one morning and go to work. He went to the hospital and died the next day. I went to my mom and felt under the bed for the father doll.... I didn't know his leaving would hurt so much."

The columnist Ellen Goodman once had the opportunity to interview Erma Bombeck when Ellen was a young reporter. Erma confessed that a reporter had once asked her how she would observe the Day of Protest against the Vietnam War.

"I told them I had three weeks of laundry I was going to do." Seated with Ellen Goodman, she worried. "Am I just sitting here while Rome burns?"

Though Erma had taken up the women's liberation movement in the sixties wholeheartedly, touring the country and speaking at rallies, one member of the women's liberation movement wrote her, saying, "Lady, you are the problem!"

Ellen Goodman saw it this way: "Erma Bombeck cracked open the feminine mystique her own way: with a sidesplitting laugh. Over the years, she wrote the truth about domestic life in all its madness and frustration, its car pools and appliances. She wrote with uncanny accuracy of the fellow traveler and a born reporter. She wrote to and about women who are, in the name of her column, 'At Wit's End.'"

She continued, "A lot of columnists write to end up in the *Congressional Record* or at the Pulitzer committee's door. But Erma Bombeck went us all one better. Her words won her the permanent place of honor in American life: the refrigerator door."

CHAPTER TWO

Haymarket Days

Even though Erma Bombeck was not born to a family that lived in the lap of luxury, she grew up in a family that faced life in a lighthearted, cheerful way. Her spirits, at least in her first years, always remained high.

She was born Erma Louise Fiste on February 21, 1927, to a mother who was also named Erma, and Cassius Edwin Fiste. Her mother was only sixteen years old at Erma's birth; she had been married when she was just fourteen. Erma also had a half sister Thelma, who was seven years old at the time of Erma's birth. Thelma was her father's daughter by his first wife.

Erma's father was a crane operator in Dayton, Ohio, where the family lived on Hedges Street. Erma was raised in a straitlaced and stern blue-collar environment. But though Cassius Fiste didn't earn much, the family was always provided for.

Erma Senior grew up in an orphanage, and went to school only through the sixth grade. In an interview many years later, Erma mistakenly said that her mother had left school after the fourth grade. Erma's mother corrected her quickly and sharply.

"You've screwed things up as usual. You said I had a fourth-grade education. That is not true. Your father had a fourth-grade education. I had a sixth-grade education."

When Erma's mother saw her chance to get married at age fourteen, she grabbed it. Though a young and inexperienced teenager, she somehow made the marriage work.

Although Erma's father was thirty-three when Erma was born—seventeen years older than her mother—the couple managed to keep the family on an even keel, even though it was weighted in the category of youth. Erma's mother was determined that her daughters would both be great successes.

The 1920s was a period of high-swinging merriment in America. World War I had loosened the country's puritanical views on sex and morality, and the sky was the limit.

Americans went on a binge of astonishing proportions—with liquor, promiscuity, and all sorts of uninhibited excesses. The stage took on a brilliance it had never known before. Motion pictures made glamorous stars of pretty young women, and girls were taught to dance at an early age.

In Erma's family there was always a stash of money set aside each week for an important expenditure—tap dancing lessons! With the country's growing enthusiasm for fun, tap dancing for youngsters paralleled social dancing for adults. Tap dancing soon became a national craze. There were tap dancing schools in Dayton, as in every other town in America.

Thelma was a very good tap dancer, and when Erma was only five years old, she began to take lessons, too. Though years later she insisted that she had never been very good at it, at that tender age she managed to win a spot on a local radio show called the *Kiddie Review*.

They aired tap dancing on radio? one might ask. The answer is yes. The great Fred Astaire starred in a network radio show for some time. He carried with him a small, low-cut box made of dance-floor oak, and when he danced on that square, he *sounded* exactly the way he did when he danced on the silver screen. People even loved to *listen* to tap dancing in those days.

Film aficionados should note that Erma was only a year older than 1934's brightest child star— Shirley Temple. Had she been in Hollywood rather than Dayton, Erma might well have become a different kind of star.

But for Erma it was quite enough to be on the radio show, tap dancing with all the other kids. She remained on the program for eight years, until she was thirteen. Besides, she was not as interested in a career on the stage as her mother was. She was dreadfully shy. She hated those first few moments when she appeared in front of people, suffering terrible stage fright.

Dancing was not the be-all and end-all of Erma's life. Erma Senior's youth inspired her daughters to play many little tricks on their mother, who was barely more than a girl herself.

Erma and Thelma would dream up antics to tease their mother when they were home from school, especially after they were put to bed. When their beds were set up on one side of the room, the kids would get up quietly after their mother had left them, and move the beds to the opposite side of the room. Then, when they were awakened in the morning, they would deny any knowledge of the move.

Silly stuff. But good for Erma. It made her first years happy and lighthearted ones—at least when Thelma was around. On weekends, when Thelma went to visit her natural mother, Erma would have to wait around and hope her sister would come back in time for a game or two. Soon enough Erma found a substitute—not a *real* substitute for a half sister, but something to occupy herself.

She found books.

With her naturally inquisitive mind, Erma had always been curious about books, and long before she went to school, she had asked her sister to read to her. She learned to read very quickly, and was hooked for life.

"As a child," she said many years later, "my number one best friend was the librarian in my grade school. I actually believed all of those books belonged to her. I would take a paper bag with me and fill it up. When she warned that some of those books were too old for me, I told her that they were for my mother. I have never regretted my dishonesty. Today the habit of reading still remains. I read no less than three books at one time. I have passed on to my children my impatience, my love of pasta—and my excitement for reading books."

Though the Great Depression made the lives of millions of people miserable, the Fistes were lucky. Erma's father kept his job, and even though the money was not great, it was adequate, and Erma's mother kept the household running smoothly.

And then it happened.

Erma was nine years old and in school. When she came home one night she learned that her father had collapsed and died of a stroke. It was later determined that he had been afflicted with adult polycystic kidney disease and had died of complications. He had never been aware that he was a sick man.

Her father's funeral was a terrible shock for Erma. Dozens of people Erma had never seen before came to pay their respects. She had never realized that her father was related to so many different people. They talked to her as if she were an old friend, patting her on the head soothingly.

She did not fully understand the implications of her father's death, of course. The times were economically bad, and more than a few families were forced to live with relatives to weather the hard times. With her father's death, the small family had lost their breadwinner.

When the excitement of the funeral subsided, Erma realized that things would never be the same in her family. Within days, movers from the department store arrived to reclaim pieces of furniture— pieces that had not yet been fully paid for. Erma had never imagined such a thing could happen, but it was happening right in front of her eyes.

"One day you were a family," she recalled, "living in a little house at the bottom of a hill. The next day it was all gone."

Her relationship with Thelma changed, too. Thelma held up through the death of her father and the funeral that followed, but she suddenly became very quiet and subdued. Erma did not understand exactly why. Then one day Thelma packed her cardboard suitcase and said good-bye to Erma and her mother. She walked down the sidewalk to the streetcar, got on, and waved good-bye again. She went to live with relatives on her mother's side of the family. It would be at least eight years before Erma saw her sister Thelma again.

Only Erma and her mother were left. The house was empty. Erma Senior told Erma that the two of them would not be living there any longer, but would be moving in with Erma's grandparents. Erma had met them before. In addition to her grandparents there were two unmarried children. No one had anything good to say about the son. He was unemployed and played pool in the neighborhood poolhalls all day. He had a sister who cleaned houses for a living. Another daughter was married and had two small children. There would be at least ten people living with her grandparents. Erma was excited. With all those people around, there would be a lot of things to talk about and a lot of games to play. And she would be living in a new neighborhood!

Erma had spent her first nine years growing up in a residential neighborhood with small houses and shops in between. But now, in her new surroundings, she was living in a much more industrial part of the city. The neighborhood was decidedly ethnic. It was called the Haymarket District of Dayton.

There were all sorts of middle European immigrants living close together in this eclectic neighborhood. A synagogue was on the corner, a Catholic church was down the street, and a group of Protestant churches were located nearby. The people were Irish, Italian, and Jewish.

The Haymarket District was what would now be called economically depressed. Winos were often found sleeping it off on the sidewalk. But Erma did not understand all the ramifications of the situation. "We were poor," she admitted later. "I'd just have been sick if I'd known. But I thought it was a really neat neighborhood. My best friend lived over the funeral parlor, and for entertainment we went to the synagogue on Saturdays and the Catholic church on Sundays—and I was a *Protestant!*"

It was exciting just living in a neighborhood like that. The people all seemed a lot more outgoing than those in her old neighborhood. They were all struggling with a new language, with a new country, and were colorful and funny in their reactions to things. Erma found herself listening to the way they spoke, amused at the grammatical mistakes, but quite taken with the original ways they expressed themselves.

And they dressed just a little differently—nothing that you could really put your finger on—and it was the difference that made them interesting. She found she could talk to them with a great deal more spontaneity than she'd ever had before.

She loved to absorb the ethnic nuances of the Haymarket District from the many immigrants and newcomers. She found them very talkative, even if they didn't know the language. And they loved to laugh—much more than her own relatives. That was the real reason she liked them so much. It was fun—great fun—just being with them.

And yet Erma felt she was cut off from the people she had always known. She was still a child, but she was aware that she would have to get used to this new life. If it was to be a lonely one, she'd make the best of it. Wasn't life a matter of making do with what one had?

Erma and her mother shared the front bedroom of her grandparents' house for the first two years of their life there. Erma missed Thelma a great deal. But there was nothing she could do. Because Erma Senior was so close in age to her daughter, they tended to relate well together and always enjoyed each other's company.

It took money to keep a household of ten people going. Soon, Erma's mother joined the multitudes desperately seeking jobs in Dayton. She was lucky. Although she had no experience, she got a job at Leland Electric Factory. Erma was very excited about her mother's job. Her mother told her she was a "stator winder." Erma later admitted, "I never knew what she really did. I never knew what a stator was." Actually, Erma's mother was winding coiled copper wire around a stator—the stationary part of a motor—around which the rotor revolves.

Later she got a job at a General Motors plant, and there she did something that Erma thoroughly understood: She threaded rubber strips around the car doors to keep the doors insulated properly.

Life was different for Erma now. She was the only girl in her class at school whose mother worked outside the home. In fact, it was hard on her to realize that when she left in the morning for school, her mother would be leaving for work too. With her mother playing an active role in bringing in money for the survival of the household, Erma sensed a feeling of desertion. She was no longer the center of her mother's world. If anything,

Erma's mother now had her own world—the world of commerce.

Though Erma felt deserted by her mother, her schoolwork did not suffer. She grew to love school. She was a quick learner, and because she was such a good reader, she was a good student as well.

Her mother was never home when she got in from school, so Erma spent her afternoons quickly doing her household chores, then grabbing a book, and settling back to read. Although some people make fun of those who read aloud to understand what they are reading, Erma loved to hear the words, as well as see them.

If there was action in the stories she read, she would act out each of the parts, as if she were reading aloud a drama. That brought the words to life for her, and made her actually see how the scenes played. It was like a very good movie!

She still kept up her tap dancing lessons, although by now Erma realized that she would never be a star. She was still dancing on the radio program, after all those years. Though she wanted to quit, Erma was afraid to tell her mother what she wanted to do with her life. Though she was only ten years old, she knew she wanted to write for the newspaper and have her stories printed. She wanted to be a writer, to excite people the way she was excited by good writing.

She knew, quite rightly, that if she ever mentioned this to her mother, she would never hear the end of it. And so she kept her dreams to herself.

CHAPTER THREE

~

A Working Daughter

When Erma was eleven years old and just getting used to living with a working mother, another change of lifestyle was suddenly thrust upon her: her mother decided to remarry. Why did she want to be married again? Erma asked herself. What was to be gained by that?

But Erma Senior was determined. She wanted a home of her own. The man she selected was Albert Harris, called "Tom" by his friends. The lifestyle change did not please Erma at all.

Tom Harris was twenty-four years old to Erma Senior's twenty-seven, and Erma Junior immediately sensed that she was going to lose her place in her mother's affections. Erma Junior was a very feisty girl for an eleven-year-old. She did not hesitate to accuse her new stepfather of trying to take over her father's place. "You can't tell me what to do," she would shout at her new father. "You're not my real father!" Which was true enough, but at the same time he *was* the head of their new household.

With her mother's remarriage, Erma Junior was suddenly cut off from the support of her family— her grandparents especially. Erma Senior and Tom Harris decided that they would move to a new house on Oak Street in Dayton—away from Erma's grandparents' home.

And so Erma found herself in a completely new environment, as well as a new lifestyle. To her, this was a disastrous move. Shouting and insulting her new stepfather seemed the only way for her to assert herself against what she considered his tyrannical attitude. That is, the attitude that he was boss. After all, Erma Senior was the real boss. Everybody knew that.

Her stepfather's immediate reaction to Erma's heat was to create a little heat of his own. What this young upstart teenager needed, he told Erma Senior, was discipline. If she could shout, he could shout, too. If she could give orders, he could give orders, too. The result was a very disordered and unhappy time for Erma and her mother. If Erma had anything to say to her stepfather, or if he had anything to say to her, each would use Erma's mother as a go-between. It was an unhappy situation for everyone.

Erma was in the eighth grade at Emerson Junior High School at the time. She liked school, her studies, the books, and the teachers, especially, but she did not get along particularly well with the rest of the students, though she did have a few friends with whom she would talk and pal around.

Somehow she could not get into the swim of things socially. The very idea of "going out" with someone was strange to her. And she did not "get in" with a set of young girls the way others did. Instead she slogged away at her schoolwork as best she could alone.

Her love of reading began to expand. She decided that she liked to read humorous things. She doted on Robert Benchley, James Thurber, and H. Allen Smith. Though she was not funny on the outside—that is, outgoing and full of jokes—she was very funny on the inside.

And she was a good, quick writer. The staff of the Emerson Junior High newspaper, *The Owl*, asked her to try her hand at writing a column, which she did. It was a humor column, naturally. And it was funny. *The Owl* took on Erma as a regular feature.

What she wrote about was, frankly, the usual: she criticized the school cafeteria's mediocre food, chastised the snooty teachers, took on the students who ran only with "in" groups, targeted the hypocrites, and so on. The quips were funny, most of them. Some were cruel and nasty, but usually there was a good laugh hidden somewhere in them. Even her critics praised her.

She had discovered that the pen was mightier than the sword—a truth that has guided writers for centuries—and she was determined to use the power of the pen to its fullest extent.

On a few occasions she was nearly expelled for what she had written, but she was always able to talk her way out of it, promising to mend her ways, which she did. Interestingly enough, her later columns, especially those that date from when her column was just beginning to be syndicated widely in the newspapers, were very similar in tone and style to those early columns she wrote in the eighth grade at Emerson Junior High School. Of course they were more thoughtful, more reasoned, and more sharply written—but they had their roots at Emerson Junior High.

By spending most of her energies on her schoolwork and writing her humor column for the paper, Erma managed to neutralize, or at least dampen, her hostility toward her stepfather. For his part, when he realized that she was not fighting him so hard, he let up on her. If she would mind her schoolwork, he would try not to make too many demands on her.

So what happened in the Harris household was a kind of truce, undeclared, between Erma Junior and Tom Harris. When Erma found that she was being attacked much less often by her stepfather, her attitude toward him changed subtly, and they began to live with one another in a much less warlike fashion.

In addition, Erma was beginning to grow up a bit herself. Being a teenager was no fun. She found herself confiding in her mother much more than before. Her mother listened to her and was very good at giving advice.

So with things going well at school and things straightening out at home, Erma began to feel as if she were living a life she wanted to live, rather than living the way someone else wanted her to. The feeling gave her a great deal of pleasure, and she realized that with such security she could get along very well anywhere.

When she finished the eighth grade at Emerson Junior High, she went on to Patterson Vocational High School, which was set up to accommodate students who would be working when they graduated. Students spent two weeks attending classes and then two weeks working. Classes ran from eight A.M. until four P.M.

Here was an excellent chance for Erma, who would be trying to get a job in the future, to acclimate herself to a work environment even as she was completing school. It all turned out very well. At the high school Erma was allowed to write her own column in journalism class, just as she had in junior high.

Her column differed just a bit. She managed to make it somewhat more serious than her humor column had been. But she did manage to sneak in a dig or two each week. She was then appointed features editor and found the environment of the journalism class much to her liking. She was beginning to spread her wings and fly.

One of the reasons for her happiness in journalism was that she had found someone who encouraged, rather than discouraged, her in her career choice. "A high school English teacher, Jim Harris, encouraged me tremendously," Erma recalled later. "He dogged me about my education."

She had her classroom schedule all set, but she had not yet landed a job for her two-week commercial alternate. She was all of fifteen years of age the day she walked in the front door of the *Dayton Journal-Herald,* found the managing editor's office, and opened the door.

The managing editor looked up and harrumphed.

"I want to work for your paper," Erma told him.

The managing editor knew all about the Patterson Vocational High School operation, and he explained patiently that he could not hire her because there was only one full-time position open on the paper at the time. He could not hire someone to work only two weeks every month.

But Erma had anticipated the objection, and had an idea. She explained that she could get another girl who was as good as she was to work the two weeks she would be at Patterson. While she was in school, Erma would work. She pointed out that in the end it would be just like having a full-time person on the paper.

The managing editor recognized spunk and determination when he spotted it. He thought it might be a good thing to have a little of it in someone on his staff. He hired her—and her alter ego.

She came on technically as a "copygirl" and "part-time secretary" at the paper. As for copy, she wrote only one or two stories the whole time she was there. Mostly she did everything all the others at the paper didn't want to do.

She mixed paste; at the time, every newspaper office used tons of paste in editing material and in re-pasting it. She ran errands, she answered the phone, she sorted and delivered the mail, and she took editors' suits to the cleaners.

In addition, every day she trotted six blocks to pick up copies of all the famous out-of-town newspapers—including all the big-city papers in the United States and Canada and all the papers from the capitals of Europe. Then she brought them back to the office and distributed them to the editorial writers.

She thrived on the newspaper environment. There was something about a newspaper that excited her more than anything else did. There was always the feeling that something was going to happen. And, since this was a newspaper, the people on staff would be the first to read about a story and see the pictures. It was a window to the world's excitement. And there were always important people coming in to see the editors and writers: politicians, especially, movers and shakers of the city, people who worked for the community, important people.

Erma was still a shy person who did not aggressively promote herself. For that reason, perhaps, she did not push herself into going out on stories. Yet one time she did have a story. She interviewed Shirley Temple, who was passing through town promoting her latest motion picture, *Since You Went Away*.

Her career did not leap forward with that story, although it was competently done and appeared in the next morning's paper. "I did it from the angle that we were both sixteen and probably had lots in common," Erma said later. "We didn't."

The story, even though it was about the most famous child star of the 1930s, didn't even make the front page. But it did win the newspaper staff award for feature of the week, and Erma earned a ten-dollar award and a spot on the bulletin board. She assured herself that this was the beginning of a great career in journalism.

Unlike many of the other girls at Patterson Vocational, Erma did not spend a great deal of her time on social matters. If anything, she simply ruled them out. Besides, nothing ever seemed to come up, anyway. She was still shy, and it seemed to work with her all right. She was not willing to sacrifice her own future to the temptations of dates with the young men at Patterson. She seemed to live a drab life, but she had steeled herself to it long before.

Besides, Erma kept her eyes wide open and observed very clearly what was going on around her. The rules of the high school society were as rigid as anything else in American society as far as she could tell. The men got all the good jobs, the good story assignments, the good beats. The women got the backup jobs and did everything no one else wanted to do. That was obvious to anyone. You kept your mouth shut and you played the game.

But Erma came from a slightly different background. Of all her schoolmates, she had been the only one whose *mother* worked. If her mother could hold down a job as well as a man could, why couldn't Erma hold down a job just as well as one of the boys in her high school class?

She never said anything about it to the people she knew, but the idea grew in her mind. And because she refused to play the dating game the way it was set up in high school, Erma became a somewhat solitary figure. She had long ago learned to live without people constantly about her. She sought solace in reading now. And what she read was humor.

Being part of a group blunted your speech, Erma found out. That is, you couldn't go around insulting people you were always with, or you would lose friends. But inhibiting yourself tended to make your conversation even duller.

She was free from this inhibition. And this allowed her to indulge her own natural bent for humor. Because she did not run with the pack, she could zero in on almost anyone she pleased, making telling comments about him or her. Erma was never nasty—but she was sharp. She pierced what humorists throughout history have pierced: hypocrisy.

And she let her schoolmates hear about it through barbed comments. The fact that what she wrote and said actually entertained a number of her peers startled her at first, until she learned that humor always was a magnet—even if it was a bit venomous. She began sharpening her comments just a bit.

Without trying to, she became a natural raconteur—someone who could always be counted on to entertain with her ironic comments on life and the people about her. In spite of the fact that she never went out of her way to become popular, she found that she was in no way unpopular—and that everyone knew her to be a witty, self-assured, and interesting young woman.

Although she never made a special effort to seek him out, Erma did meet a young man on the newspaper who interested her very much. His name was William Lawrence Bombeck—and everyone called him Bill.

Bill was a copyboy, just as Erma was a copygirl. He actually went to the Catholic high school, and worked on the morning paper as part of his schedule. He was interested in journalism, too, he told her, and hoped to make a career of it someday.

"We had the most exciting jobs around," Erma recalled. "He was covering high school sports and I was on features, radio listings, and obituaries."

Bill wasn't unaware of Erma's interest in him. He knew her reputation—knew that she did not go the general dating route. As for Bill, he divided his time between about a half dozen girls, picking and selecting as the weeks wore on.

In their senior year, Erma and Bill dated several times, but to Bill it was just as casual as his other dates, and to Erma, it was fun while it lasted. Quite suddenly, Bill was eligible for the draft. World War II was still on, and Bill Bombeck signed up for army service, and was gone in 1945.

Erma graduated from high school in 1944, and wanted to go to college. However, the Harris family didn't have enough money to pay for a college education for Erma Fiste—even though college fees were nowhere near as high as they are in the 1990s.

"Your goals were supposed to be modest," Erma recalled. "If you were a girl, you either got a job and paid board, or you got married." She was a working-class girl, while only middle-class teenagers went on to college from high school in those days. But for most girls, college was seen as a kind of lark between high school graduation and marriage, except for a few who planned to become professionals or teachers.

That was the way the game was played—and

Erma was one of the female players, at a disadvantage, as usual. Nevertheless, she was incensed over the fact that, in part because she was a girl, her parents would not pay for her college education. But she knew how it was. She decided that she would simply have to earn her own living and, if she could, get through college on her own. However, this decision left a bitterness between her parents and her that took years to wear off.

By the time she had made the decision to attend college, it was too late for her to apply for the fall, so Erma decided to get a job and start saving her money. The *Dayton Journal-Herald* was glad to have her back. They promoted her from part-time to full-time copygirl. She stayed for a year—involved mostly in knocking out obituaries.

It was there that she met Phyllis Battelle, a newspaperwoman who went on to become a famous syndicated columnist. The first time she met her, Battelle knew that Erma was going to be someone in the business. In fact, she remembered her vividly as "a bouncy kid in bobbysocks, knife-pleated skirts, and baggy sweaters."

In her heart, Battelle knew that Erma Fiste was a superior article. She joked, "She was destined to go places even back then—usually to the arcade around the corner, to buy coffee and sweet rolls for editors."

Battelle continued, "We didn't realize at the time that under the tawny curls there resided the whacko psyche of a young genius who could find humor in everything. Especially in life's tragedies and drudgeries."

Erma worked at night as well, trying to earn money for her education. She worked at Wright-Patterson Air Force Base editing proofs on airplane manuals, which paid even more than her job at the newspaper.

By the end of the year she had enough money to start college. She enrolled at Ohio University in Athens, Ohio, over a hundred miles from her home.

CHAPTER FOUR

"You Can Write!"

Whatever her expectations for her first semester in college were, they could not have been lower than what actually happened—or didn't happen—to her. In short, her freshman semester at the University of Ohio was an unmitigated disaster. She did not flunk out, but she performed on such a low level of competence, according to her professors, that she might just as well have never enrolled.

While Erma was a gutsy young woman, she did not know everything there was to know about the world outside of her home. She may have thought she did, but she did not. It was perhaps simply a case of her having expected one thing in college and having found quite another.

Until 1945—the year she enrolled as a freshman at Ohio—her teachers had always praised her work, especially in English. They had been extravagant in their compliments on her other accomplishments, too. She did well in history, in geography, in mathematics, and in science. But somehow, when she started fresh at the University of Ohio, she was no longer the A student she had been.

It occurred to her that she just wasn't smart enough to go to college. Her high school teachers had been kidding her. She couldn't figure out what her college professors expected of her. She gave them the same thing she had given her high school teachers, and they rarely marked her higher than a C—sometimes, to her distinct displeasure, she got lower than a C.

Her best subject was now her worst. She wasn't even sure she would pass her freshman course in English composition. In fact, because she was Erma, she began arguing with her professor about what "good literature" really was. To make matters worse, she sent a number of articles she had written to the school paper in order to get a job there, but she was rejected.

It was astonishing to Erma that she had worked on a *real* newspaper for four years, but now could not write a story that would appear in a college newspaper! Her writing simply was not good enough. What was wrong with her? How had she made this egregious error in choosing a profession for which she was simply not fit?

Besides these problems, which were entirely new in her life, Erma was lonely so far away from home. The fact that she had taken off on her own, and had not followed the advice of her parents, galled her in addition to the fact that she was lonely. The entire plan had been a disaster. She would have to decide what to do—and do it immediately.

When her first semester ended and her shameful grades lay before her, she immediately got an interview with an academic counselor to try to find out what was wrong. The counselor asked her the obvious question: "What do you want to do with your life?" When Erma replied that she wanted to be a writer, he took one look at her grades and shook his head. "Don't even try it."

Erma was reduced to a shocked silence. She had always wanted to write. She thought she was good at it. But if it was obvious to the world that she was not as bright as she thought, she would have to lower her professional sights somewhat.

Here it was only the middle of her first year in college; she had fought a battle with her parents even to be in Athens at the University of Ohio. Now it was obvious that things had not worked out for her. It would be sensible to swallow her pride and quit, pack up her things, and go home to Dayton.

No! she finally said to herself. She had gotten a job with three professors in the science department to help her work her way through college. She knew that the people back in Dayton at the newspaper were behind her. They thought she was good at what she was doing there. If they all supported her, why should she quit?

But, if she wasn't going to be a successful writer, what was she going to be? The answer to that question stumped her. In the back of her mind Erma knew that her mother was still miffed at her for dropping her tap dancing career. If she fled home now in disgrace, what could she expect but to be ordered to put on her tap dancing shoes and do what her mother had planned for her to do from the beginning? Become another Shirley Temple!

And yet Erma was enough of a realist to realize that a tap dancing career was even harder to break into than newspaper reporting.

To Erma's mother, the very idea of being a writer was boring. She thought the glamorous life would be seeing her daughter's face on the cover of every movie magazine in town—or at least on the posters in front of the theaters where her daughter would be performing. That was fame! That was the glamorous life of a star!

Despondent, Erma telephoned her mother and had a heart-to-heart talk. Erma did not admit that she had been wrong to insist on coming to the University of Ohio. But she did admit that her grades were not as high as she had expected. She almost admitted to her mother that she had blown it.

Oddly enough, her mother sympathized with her, and, instead of lecturing her, said she was sorry to hear it and that maybe Erma had better drop out of the university and come home for a while. The "for a while" absolutely floored Erma. Her mother was giving her a second chance! And she took it.

Erma packed her bags that night, and the next day was on her way back home. She had no idea what she was going to do to resurrect her failed career. But she knew that she still wanted to be a writer.

Her arrival at home did not lift her spirits any. The battle of mother and daughter resumed as soon as she had settled in. Her stepfather tempered himself somewhat, but he still let her know how he felt about her misadventure at Athens. The scene was not a happy one.

But then Erma's ability to turn the darkest day into a sunny one came to her rescue. There was a private, medium-sized, four-year Catholic college in the middle of town—the University of Dayton. Erma looked over the curriculum and decided to enroll. She knew she would have to work at the same time, so she arranged her schedule so that it included only morning classes. In the afternoon and on weekends she could work at outside jobs in order to earn money for her courses.

She got a full-time job at Rake's Department Store, where she edited a newsletter that was distributed among the employees for their amusement. As usual, she made the material into humorous features—the lousy food on the lunch menu, behind the scenes at clearance sales, and even a story or two about shoplifting at the store. She also got two part-time jobs—a termite control account at an advertising agency and a public relations job at the local YMCA.

She most enjoyed the newsletter work. "You can't imagine how [the stuff I wrote] fractured those people," she said years later. "I knew exactly what I wanted to do. I wanted to write. That's all I wanted to do. I really loved the exaggeration. I still write about passing my varicose veins off as textured stockings."

In a business sense, Erma knew how to hustle. She now made good use of her talents, for she was working against time—four years of a college curriculum.

In 1946 she settled in at the University of Dayton quickly and easily. She had decided to begin as a freshman, as if she had never attended the University of Ohio. The campus itself was quite a contrast to the more energetic, pushy, crowded campus at Athens. This was a quiet, hospitable place, a sanctuary of sorts, a hiding place from the rough and tumble world that lay just outside its borders.

Her parents did not actually see her move to the University of Dayton as productive, but since she did not make any requests for money or help of any kind, they left her alone.

For some reason, the entire lifestyle at the

University of Dayton turned things around for Erma. It may have been the quiet and relaxed atmosphere that permeated the place. Whatever the reason, Erma flourished there.

First, her grades improved immeasurably. Second, she began to hear compliments on her writing style once again—something that had been missing at the University of Ohio. And third, she began to find that working her way through college was not as much an indignity and hardship as she had thought it might be. Besides, she not only liked her courses at the University but she liked her three jobs, too.

During her sophomore year at the University of Dayton, in 1947, she began to find herself. She had been producing a number of pieces for the university newspaper—all of which had been printed— and one of the professors, Brother Tom Price, was looking for writing talent to provide material for the University of Dayton's magazine, *The Exponent*. He asked Erma to write a few things for him.

Erma was thrilled that someone she respected had actually liked her writing. She applied herself seriously to the typewriter and wrote a number of a magazine pieces for him.

Without realizing it, she had grown up during

the time she had been in Athens and had started working her way through the University of Dayton. She was also incorporating the material she had read in her university courses—points on psychology and sociology—which made her writing just a bit more mature than it had been before.

After Brother Tom Price read one of her articles for *The Exponent,* he nodded and said only three words. "You can write!" And then he repeated it. "You can write!"

For Erma, those three words solidified her dedication to a life of writing and gave her faith in herself whenever she began to lack it. In her heart she now felt that she was on her way to a career in journalism.

In 1948, Bill Bombeck returned from Korea. His three-year hitch had been served, and he was a civilian once again. But he had lost three college years by joining the army, and now needed to play catch-up.

Bill and Erma had pursued a rather vigorous correspondence over the years, and when he returned home, Bill began pursuing a much more serious relationship with Erma Fiste. Bill's renewed presence in her life convinced Erma that his intentions were serious. At this time, she realized that she had another issue with which to deal. Throughout her career at the University of Dayton she had been gradually turning to the Catholic Church for solace. Now, with Bill, a Catholic, so close to her, Erma began to plan how she would tell her mother and father that she wanted to convert from Protestantism to Roman Catholicism.

This was, of course, a very serious matter. Before letting anyone know that she was even thinking of changing her religion, she wrestled with her decision for months. She had joined the United Brethren Church in Dayton and had been a good Protestant for years. But she had always lived in a multiethnic neighborhood in which there were Catholics and Jews as well as almost every other religious denomination.

"I saw something in it I wanted to have," she told *Time* magazine in 1984. "There is something very soothing about the whole thing. A love of God is easier for me to accept than the fear." There were bits and pieces of the Catholic doctrine that were hard for her to take—as they were for scores of other Catholics. The usual issues of reproduction always bothered her. She agreed with the prohibition of abortion, but could never accept the strictures against birth control.

But she thought at length about her beliefs, and decided finally that she would initiate another strong act of independence from her family. In 1949, at the age of twenty-one, she became a Roman Catholic.

Nineteen-forty-nine was a year of great change for Erma. First, she graduated with a B.A. in English from the University of Dayton. Then, on August 13, she and Bill Bombeck were married.

Both Erma and Bill were twenty-one years old. They were married at the Church of the Resurrection, with Erma wearing an organza gown. It was an oversized frock that she had bought on sale. The buyer from Rike's Department Store had sold her the dress at a huge discount, and the store's seamstress had altered it for her for free.

What Erma remembered most was the fact that her mother had baked a ham to take to the reception, and every time her mother came near, Erma could smell the baked ham on her. It was an overcast and threatening day; but what might have been an ominous sign to anyone else was cast aside by Erma, who was determined that this would be a successful and memorable wedding.

There were a hundred and fifty people in attendance. Most of them were relatives. When Erma first saw her husband-to-be, she noticed immediately that he had a spot of white paint on his ear. She could smell the faint but penetrating odor of turpentine. After all, Bill did paint houses in his extra time to supplement his income.

To top things off, one of the bridesmaids fainted in the middle of the mass. She had not bothered to eat any breakfast, and, being Protestant, had no idea how long the mass was going to take.

The best man was Bill's friend Ed Phillips. He remembered the ring, and everything was finally going well. Erma was straining her ears to try to make out what the priest was saying. He was Polish and spoke half his words in the Latin of the mass. But she did hear the words: "You, Bill, are to be the head of the house and you, Erma, are to be the heart."

"In his dreams!" Erma wrote later in reaction to the priest's words. But soon the priest was intoning the portentous words: "I now pronounce you man and wife." And they were married.

Erma recalled that one of the guests asked her where they were going on their honeymoon. Erma told her that she wanted to go to New York City, see a Broadway show, and stay at a fancy hotel. Then she and Bill would ride through Central Park in a carriage. The honeymoon actually took place at Sunny Lake Ranch in Michigan. Erma's private name for Sunny Lake Ranch was Larvae Lake.

In the middle of the reception, Erma and Bill sneaked away in Bill's sister's car and headed for Sunny Lake Ranch. When they got there, the first thing Erma saw were bear traps outside the cabin they had rented. "That's it!" she said. "That's it! I'm out of here."

But she stayed. And so began a long and happy marriage.

CHAPTER FIVE

∾

Suburbia Meets Erma

It was a time of many changes in the lives of Erma and Bill Bombeck. Not only had Erma converted from Protestantism to Roman Catholicism but she had also graduated from college and gotten married. In addition, Erma began a new job at the *Dayton Journal-Herald,* who took her on as a full-time newspaperwoman.

Though Bill had accelerated his college career, he still had one full year to go. He would be taking courses while Erma was working; in effect, she would be supporting him while he finished college. He had switched from journalism to education as a major in the interim, and he hoped to find a job in the Dayton school system. Journalism, he had decided, was too hard a profession to crack.

Erma had no such qualms about journalism. She knew she was much less ambitious than Bill, and she accepted that fact. And so she did not complain when her first assignment as a full-time staffer on the *Dayton Journal-Herald* turned out to be the tedious chore of writing obituaries. Although this was no journalist's idea of working on a newspaper, she gritted her teeth and turned out dozens of pieces for her bosses—as she had done before.

Occasionally she was given a reporting assignment, but it would inevitably be covering a garden club meeting, or some other "female-oriented" story. She knew zilch about cooking; her mother could attest to that. She didn't know too much about housekeeping either, nor was she even interested in it. Unfortunately, those were the only stories usually available to a female reporter.

Deep in her heart, Erma knew she was a fraud. That is, she knew that being a top-notch journalist was not her calling. Facts kept getting in the way of good prose and witty insights. She even admitted once, "I was terrible at straight items. When I wrote obituaries, my mother said the only thing I ever got them to do was die in alphabetical order." She had taken shorthand in college, and while she was good at it, it didn't help her as a reporter. "I could never get the knack of listening and taking notes at the same time."

There were problems with her story slants, too. For example, she once accompanied a group of teenagers on a class trip to Washington and New York. Erma palled around with the kids, listening to their lingo and getting quotes from them. It was the year the Russian Embassy opened, and the fete there was an important one. Erma was enthusiastic about it, and she wrote it up from the point of view of the teenagers she was with. Her boss was less enthusiastic: "You covered that like a tea party." Erma had to admit that her boss was right. Her story was ridiculous. But she had followed her instincts. Obviously, her instincts were pointing away from top-notch, arresting, front-page newspaper copy.

Her more successful stories were mostly about social events that could be described as "women's affairs"—society features, weddings, and women's features of all shapes and sizes. Erma once confessed, "I never took a note so whoever I interviewed—even Eleanor Roosevelt—came out sounding just like me." Because, of course, it *was* Erma all the time!

The humor kept sneaking back in. She couldn't entirely wipe it out, although she was cautioned time and again by her mentors. As she put it, "Every once in a while I tried to inject a humorous personal story—about some domestic thing such as going on a vacation—but newspapers were not very receptive to humor in the 1940s. Occasionally a humorous story [of mine] would run."

As was almost inevitable, Erma wound up doing a women's page column with elements of humor allowed to surface here and there. She was, she recalled later, "a sort of sick Heloise.... I told people to go clean their johns, lock them up, and send the kids to the gas station at the corner."

The column came to be known as "Operation Dustrag"—a more or less humorous sampling of housework as seen by Erma Bombeck. "I took on housework, if you can make housework humorous," she said.

This column, humorous though it was with fine little spots of Bombeck humor here and there, was pretty much lost on the readers of the time. These were the days before the Equal Rights Amendment had become important to feminists. The column never caught fire, and the in-box was not crammed with appreciative letters from fans. Frankly, it was something of a dud.

There was good reason for this. The years following World War II were not years in which it was de rigueur to make fun of domestic chores. "Housework," Erma explained, "was a religious experience!"

In effect, it was considered an art to be able to manage a home correctly—with no traces of gunk, no dust balls in the corner, no evidence of anything but cleanliness and godliness showing through to anyone on the outside.

Erma's sly glance at housework was almost a first—if not a true first. With a bit of luck, Erma could have made "Operation Dustrag" work, because the *need* for her attitude was there, festering inside women.

World War II had changed the world forever—especially the United States. Housewives who had never worked before took industry jobs during the war. Women were no longer the captives of the household. That joy that came with receiving a paycheck did not go away when the war ended; a lot of women simply did not go back to the confines of housekeeping, but continued to work when the war was over.

Things were changing, and the women who opted to stay home knew it. Their outlooks were already beginning to change. Erma, along with other writers, saw it at first, but they were unable to get their readers to see it as clearly as they did. It would just take time for the rest of the world to catch up with them.

Meanwhile, Bill Bombeck had graduated from the University of Dayton with a B.A. in Education. He got a job as a science teacher at Centerville High School, in a suburb of Dayton. When Bill came home with the news of his job, they decided that Erma would quit her job to become a home-maker as soon as their first child arrived. She had always thought that marriage meant a family; and family, of course, meant having kids.

By dint of working on a tight budget, the Bombecks managed to make due with very little while putting some money into savings. But the bills kept coming in, and both Bombecks kept working to pay them.

Bill's job as a science teacher was somewhat un-conventional. He said, "I was teaching everything back then: spelling, science, English, history, sociol-ogy, government, and arithmetic."

As for Erma, deep down, she was getting just plain bored with her steady job. Instead of writing front-page stories, she was doing women's page stuff and obituaries. She admitted, "I was sick of working. Putting on panty hose every morning is just not whoopee time. My dream was to putter around the house, learn how to snap beans, put up curtains, and bake bread."

Yet Erma continued at the paper, though it was more or less a waiting game. She would be having a family, and as soon as that happened, she would say good-bye to her colleagues and move to Centerville to become a homemaker, Centerville being a new suburban development a few miles from Dayton.

Wanting to have a child was no joke to Erma. She may have laughed at neighbors and friends who flashed pictures of their kids at every opportunity, talking ceaselessly about their broods—but deep in her heart she wanted children, too. She wanted to be a mother.

And yet, after two years of waiting, nothing was happening. She began visiting doctors to find out if something was preventing conception. The family doctor told her that her chances of conceiving were infinitesimally small.

Erma later admitted that she and Bill did not talk to each other about the problem that existed, even though it was the most important part of their marriage. She felt that neither of them wanted to blame the other in any way for the event that was not happening.

The toughest things to face, Erma said, were the times when they heard that friends were expecting. Bill always assured his friends that they were very lucky people and that he envied them. Erma said that she tried acting as if she were glad *they* were the ones it was happening to, not her.

Of course these were very bad days for Erma. She became more impatient than ever before— impatient to have a baby. She wanted to have a baby when all her friends were having theirs. Anything else would be unbearable. She imagined her life without children. It would be a ghastly, lonely existence—even with Bill there. He, too, would be thinking about the children they never had. It was enough to make Erma weep.

Instead of waiting for their luck to change, the Bombecks decided to adopt a child. But first, a social worker would need to examine their lifestyle in detail. They seemed to pass the test. Both were working, but of course Erma would quit her job when the child was adopted. After a series of exhaustive interviews, the social worker said that quite possibly the Bombecks could have a child within two years or so.

In the end, it wasn't quite two years—but it *seemed* like more. The interviews by the social worker continued. One lazy Saturday afternoon, Bill was laid up with a nasty case of poison oak on his legs. Relaxing with a beer in hand, he soaked his legs in a beer cooler full of solution while watching a football game. Erma, meanwhile, was attempting to fashion a room divider with a plastic pink closeline, weighing it down with a planter full of rocks. Naturally, the social worker chose that afternoon to make a surprise inspection. Red-faced, Erma welcomed her in, certain that their odyssey to adopt had come to an abrupt end. Imagine her surprise to learn that they had passed the test with flying colors!

Soon after New Year's Day, 1954, the social worker rang them up with good news and soon arrived to introduce them to a seven-month-old little girl with blue eyes, telling them to "be happy." And so Betsy became the Bombecks' first child.

Erma's friends were happy for her, but they let some of their feelings seep out when they talked to her. They were annoyed that Erma had never experienced the usual heartburn accompanying pregnancy, had never had to force her bloated stomach under a steering wheel, and had never had her water break in the middle of the night.

It was too simple! Just strip open the package, add formula, and stir—you're a mother.

But nothing really mattered to the Bombecks except that Betsy had come into their lives—and, for the first time, the Bombeck family felt complete.

Of course, Erma's entire lifestyle changed from that moment on. In spite of the fact that she had never carried the baby in her body, the entire house now became a baby-supporting structure. The nights were filled with squalls and outbursts, with plenty of time spent getting Betsy back to sleep. The days were full of sterilizing, heating, changing, burping, and rocking.

True to her original promise, once Betsy was established in the household, Erma quit her job on the paper to spend all her time in the house. It was a good thing she had decided to do so, for in 1955, in spite of what her doctor had told her, Erma bore her first son, Andy. Three years later, in 1958, Matthew was born, to complete the family.

During Erma's pregnancy with Andy, the Bombecks

finally attained their dream—they bought a small home in Centerville just outside Dayton, on a street called Cushwa Drive. Erma often wisecracked that it seemed to have been named for some dentist.

The house's big sale's feature was a two-way fireplace in the center of the house that opened onto the living room and an area at the rear. Nobody informed the Bombecks that this type of fireplace was quite common in those postwar years of suburban construction.

In addition to the two-way fireplace, their front door was painted red. Erma swore it was so that Erma Senior and Tom Harris could find them when they visited the crowded development and got lost in its winding streets.

The Bombecks settled into suburbia quite easily. Bill Bombeck had always been a tinkerer, and now he tinkered around the new house. He also became a handyman for the neighborhood, making a little extra money to augment his rather skimpy teacher's paycheck by doing his usual housepainting chore for his more affluent and less ambitious neighbors. He also had another job at the post office during school vacations.

Bill also mowed the front lawn, the same way millions of homeowners all across America in the heyday of the new suburbia mowed theirs each weekend. Since suburbia depended on wheels, the Bombecks bought a car immediately after signing the mortgage papers for the house. The Bombecks were now bona fide suburbanites.

Erma spent her time doing all the things a housewife does, while repainting, redecorating, and rearranging the furniture. These developed into homemaking years—monotonous ones to be sure but definitely important to Erma Bombeck, who lived through it all with wide-open eyes and a memory that duly recorded all the absurd and idiotic things that happened around her.

She was philosophical about her years as a home-maker. She loved having kids and loved bringing them up. The peskiness of housework was some-thing she came to abhor yet could not really get rid of. But while she was sometimes sarcastic about homemaking chores and things that had to be done around the house, she did not ever sneer at the homemaking years in general. They were extremely important to her. These years were much more than simply marking time and waiting for the inevitable moment when she would be able to fly back into journalism.

She did everything she could to be the best

homemaker she could be. "I really worked on it for a very long time," she said. Once Betsy, her daughter, asked her how she could *stand* doing it. She answered, "I worked hard at it."

She recalled, "I would take decorating classes. I would crochet little knobs for the doorknobs with Santa Claus and whiskers. I'd make taffy for the kids, take them on field trips. Volunteered like crazy. I just kept very busy.

"It was a lot of fun," she said. "I even enjoyed scrubbing an occasional floor."

Erma had always wanted to give her kids the secure childhood that she herself had missed. She explained it this way: "I was overwhelmed. You get from your mother what things should be. I'm killing myself. We all did. Are you ready for this? I'm sitting there at midnight bending a coat hanger, putting nose tissue on it to make a Christmas wreath for the door. You know what it looks like? It looks like a coat hanger with tissue that is going to melt when it rains. It's a desperation you cannot imagine.

"I had a husband who worked at his job until seven or eight P.M. taking care of other people's children. That's when I remember reading Jean Kerr, who would sit in her car and hide, reading the car-manual section on tire pressure. It's ridiculous. The whole thing is ridiculous. It's the core of laughter. If you can't make it better, you can laugh at it."

And laugh she did. She once quipped, "If the Virgin Mary had lived on our block, we would have said, 'Of course she had time to go to the dentist. She only has Jesus.'"

She was quick to put the life of a homemaker in its proper perspective: "It is not as good as anyone, including your mother, promised it would be. It is also as good as it is ever going to get. And no matter what you do, no one is ever going to thank you."

CHAPTER SIX

∾

"At Wit's End"

From the moment when Erma and Bill Bombeck became the parents of Betsy Bombeck, their lives changed drastically. The entire house was taken over with children's accessories: food, beverages, and toys. There was no room any longer for Erma and Bill—or so it seemed.

As Erma wrote so poignantly in 1993, "I was no longer 'Erma.' I was somebody's mother. I would have been someone's wife had I not been ironing or packing lunches at eleven P.M."

She was in charge of the household, and that meant that she was at least 90 percent in charge of Betsy, and, later on, Andy and Matthew. Erma's private life was entirely on hold. Her waking hours—and perhaps her sleeping hours as well— were filled ministering to her children's needs. She understood the necessities of child-rearing, and she knew very well that she had made a vow to God to quit work and take care of her kids if she were able to have them. She simply faced the situation without any regrets—at least on the surface.

But motherhood, she discovered, was a demanding responsibility. Now, with three children, there was no longer any Erma, as she had written. There was only "mom." For the woman who had grown up believing firmly that she would be an ace reporter for *The New York Times,* it was ironic that she did not even have enough time to read the paper anymore. While her plans for *The New York Times* receded into the background, her dream of writing did not.

She said, "I had my dreams in the back of my mind," but she dared not reveal them to anyone else because they were fragile and might break. "I wanted to return to writing, but what if I tried and failed? Then I would have nothing left to hang on to."

In Centerville, Bill was teaching science at the high school. Erma, with her penchant for moonlighting, soon finagled a job with the *Dayton Shopping News* as editor of the whole paper. A shopping throwaway, the *News* was scarcely a breakthrough to the big time, but it was a chance for Erma to indulge herself in what she wanted to do most—write.

Unfortunately, there was little text in the paper, since it dealt mostly in big advertising spreads. But Erma managed to take on public relations jobs for various firms to fill up the pages of the *News* with copy. She did jobs for the YWCA and wrote stories covering its activities to publicize the organization.

"You have to dream to write humor," Erma said once. "It is a matter of looking at tragedy and dreaming up some humor in it. That way, you survive. If you don't take yourself seriously, it's sure as heck you're not going to take anything else seriously."

Her philosophy helped her in her editing of the *Dayton Shopping News*. Her sense of humor was maturing. She was much less apt to use a scathing sarcastic phrase now than when she had been writing for the college audience. And she saw the world from the point of view of the kitchen and dining room rather than a classroom or a politician's podium.

As she was pondering her role as homemaker and her secret career as writer, Erma spotted her new neighbor trying to dislodge a diaper from his new toilet. She learned that the man's name was Phil Donahue, and that he was just starting a job as a local television news reporter. Though their conversation is unfortunately lost to history, she did certainly welcome him to the joys of the burbs. In her heart though, Erma wondered, "Donahue can do it. Why can't I?"

She was still wondering this in 1963 when her last child, Matthew, finally entered kindergarten. With all the kids out of the house in the morning, Erma now had a chance to take a deep breath and get her life a little more in focus. And as she looked around she saw with dreadful clarity exactly what she had become: an interchangeable cog in the great juggernaut of suburbia.

"You get so you think you can't do anything but get stains out of bibs," she said. She realized that she was looking dreamily at the ads in the magazines that said EARN MONEY—ADDRESS ENVELOPES AT ONE CENT APIECE. She was wondering, Could I do that? She knew she had to do something to enhance her life. Something like join a club, get a job—but she simply had to have something *else* to do. "I was thirty-seven—too old for a paper route, too young for social security, and too tired for an affair."

She was exactly like every other woman whose children were growing up, wondering whether or not she could take the plunge and go back to work. "It's awful," she said. "You lie to yourself. The truth is, you're scared you might fall on your face and that would be your last shot, lady."

It was a combination of things that finally got Erma to change her life. Partially, it was the growing success of her neighbor Phil Donahue. He was doing all right, and here he was in the same neighborhood! And there was the problem of the *Dayton Shopping News*. Editing was all right, but the little writing she was able to slip in did not satisfy her ambitions.

She knew she could make people laugh. She was still as funny as she had been when she was in school. Even funnier, now that suburbia was beginning to be examined critically. Why couldn't she get people to laugh at what was around them? After all, she was a housewife, she was a homemaker, and she was a mother. There were women in the same situation next door, down the street, across the way, around the block. That was what she wanted to write about. The house and the kids. "I found much of it funny, and human, so I decided to write about it."

Erma Bombeck sat down in front of her battered portable typewriter and hammered out a number of pieces to show to local editors. She knew what was funny and what wasn't. She knew she could sell herself—or at least she hoped she could.

In 1964, Erma Bombeck took a very deep breath and knocked on the door of Ron Ginger, the editor of the *Kettering-Oakwood Times*. The *Times* was a weekly newspaper with a circulation of about twelve thousand. The newspaper served the Dayton suburbs.

The editor read her pieces and thought them over. He was not too enthusiastic about a housewifey column, although he knew it might prove popular among his readers. He could see that Erma had a good sense of humor, though, and at the last minute, instead of handing them back to her with a curt no, he paused and read through one of them again. "Okay," he said. And the two of them began planning what the column she was to write would be called. In the end it became known simply as "Zone 59," which was Centerville's post office code. "Zone 59" would appear once a week, and Erma would be paid three dollars for each column.

After a few issues of the paper had carried Erma's new column, the reaction was uniformly positive. There were no raves, but it was definitely a noticed and liked column.

Erma was still developing her writing style. Her columns generally featured local people who had interesting occupations or pastimes. Once, she was assigned to write a story about a local football game for the news department. An editor recalled, "She wrote a hilarious piece about the people in the stands, and handled the game itself in the final paragraph." It wasn't exactly what the news department wanted, but the paper ran it away.

In another instance, she wrote a "pretend" letter to the editor, complaining about an imaginary exterminator supposedly advertised in the newspaper.

"When you showed ants screaming hysterically, clutching their throats and eventually falling dead while a tombstone and large flower arose out of their chest, I knew this was exaggerated.... However, I don't feel I'm unreasonable to expect just one of our ants to stagger or cough however inaudibly. After distributing your product throughout, I observed them at some length and they are gobbling up the poison like Swedish meatballs at an eleven P.M. dinner party.... I fully expect them to ask for 'doggie bags' to take away what they can't eat under the table...."

Erma was in control of her material to a degree she had never been before. She was getting ready to break into the big time—or at least, it looked that way. She wrote the column for about a year and a half. And in that year and a half a lot of people took notice.

One of them was a man named Glenn Thompson. Thompson was the executive editor of the *Dayton Journal-Herald*—Erma Bombeck's old stomping grounds when she had been a journalist.

Thompson was intrigued by what he saw in her columns and wrote her a letter. This is the way Erma remembers it: "I didn't know him. We had never met, but if there is one person in this world who is responsible for what I have done, it's that man. I got a letter from him saying he'd like me to write a regular humor column for his editorial page. Without further ado, he signed me up to do three columns a week."

The title of the column was to be "At Wit's End." And for "At Wit's End," Erma would get a huge raise—fifteen dollars apiece for three columns a week, or twelve dollars more per column than she had earned at the *Times*. That was a 400 percent raise. With that kind of a future, who knew where it would all end?

Thompson recalled, "[Ron] Ginger was a friend of mine, so I had warned him that I was going to steal his columnist. He was pleased that Erma would be doing better. It didn't take me long to satisfy myself that Erma could be funny three times a week."

Within three weeks Thompson put together a batch of Erma Bombeck's columns and sent them to Tom Dorsey at Newsday Syndicate on Long Island, New York. The columns intrigued Dorsey as well as Thompson. Thompson told the story: "Tom went to Dayton and had dinner with Erma and me." Dorsey told Erma that she was in tune with suburban women all over the country. Thompson said, "You've got to give her a bigger audience." Dorsey agreed. Newsday Syndicate took Erma on in 1965 with a three-times-a-week column titled "At Wit's End," as one of the Newsday Specials.

An excited Erma told her family at the dinner table that night that she was going to be a newspaper star. There was silence. No one stopped eating. No one said anything. Then, finally, Betsy looked up, somewhat disgruntled. "Does this mean you can't take me to Scouts on Tuesday?"

The Newsday Syndicate's pitch for Bombeck's

column served as an introduction for Erma's column. After explaining that the humor column by a young suburban housewife would appear three times a week—Sunday, Tuesday, and Thursday—the copy went on to say that she had three kids and a husband in Centerville, Ohio.

The copy then quoted from a column Erma wrote about taking the kids to a movie, "We both agreed we had seen so many Flipper episodes, we had to buy nose plugs! At any rate, it came out my turn and there I was standing in a cold line that snaked to the outskirts of town. The kids were running in and out of shops with food that was to be the beginning of a four-hour snack-a-thon. And, once inside the theater, they were busier than a fly in a fruitcake."

Also included was a quote about checking books out of the library that reflected the rather puritanical outlook on life in 1950s America. "When you live in a small community where the librarian knows you by your first name, your blood type, and your record club serial number, you can't be too careful about the books you read. I, for one, don't want to be referred to behind the book stalls as 'Old Smutty Tongue.'"

The piece then quoted Erma's descriptions of her

housing development, "You sneeze and they say gesundheit three doors away," and a dog they once had, "Stupid? He couldn't find his way back from the mailbox."

The pitch gave some biographical details of Erma's life, and then claimed she was not a typical suburbanite because she hadn't yet lost her identity "as the women's magazines say [I] should have." "I do my own housework (carp about it hourly), take oil painting lessons, and handle the family budget (which is why we move a lot)."

She explained away the odd spelling of her first name. "I think I just come from a family of poor spellers." When an editor once chided her for misspelling the word "inauguration," she remarked, "Oh, well, I have plenty of time to look it up. It won't happen again for four years."

Her children, she said, never read her columns, which she wrote in the bedroom. "They say you can tell what your kids think of you by the presents they give. For Christmas I got a pot holder, a box of iron-on patches, and a hairbrush."

Erma recalled her journalistic breakthrough with characteristic aplomb. "I did nothing. I just watched it all happen."

Less than a month after her first column appeared in the *Dayton Journal-Herald,* she signed a contract with the Newsday Syndicate—which had been arranged by Thompson. And now Thompson had the last laugh on her. Syndication rates depend upon newspaper circulation rates, with the widely distributed papers costing more than the locally distributed ones.

"I had been paying $45 a week for Erma," Thompson chuckled. "When the syndicate took her over, I was able to buy her for only $15."

But this was hardly bad news for Erma. Thirty-eight papers were buying her column by the end of the first year of syndication, a surefire indication of success.

Within five years, "At Wit's End" was a regular column in 500 newspapers. Much later, in 1988, she would move her column to Universal Press Syndicate. During the years between her dramatic debut and 1988, she would bounce from one syndicate to another, depending on the advantages and the revenues of each, but the move to Universal Press Syndicate was one of the best deals she ever made.

UPS eventually distributed Erma to more than 700 newspapers. It was the biggest independent syndicate in the country, and the third or fourth largest of all the syndicates. Erma could reach more people through UPS than through any other syndicate at the time.

Like most other syndicated columns, Erma's ran about 400 to 500 words, with very little deviation. Newspapers could cut copy if they had to, but Erma always managed to deliver her columns well within the mandated length.

Her success was a sudden and dizzying one, in spite of the fact that she had been writing columns most of her life. It was as if the world had been waiting for the right moment to celebrate her. And now, in 1965, with the chaos of John F. Kennedy's assassination finally beginning to subside and the revolution of the 1960s solidifying in the national consciousness, it was time for Erma's raised-eyebrow look at the suburban dream.

CHAPTER SEVEN

Author, Author!

In general, the only books anyone ever hears about are the enormous best-sellers, quite frequently penned by some famous basketball player or celebrity. No one notices that the majority of books are *not* best-sellers, and are but mediocre sellers at best—books that have a short shelf life before being relegated to obscurity.

Nevertheless, in spite of the fact that best-sellers are rare, the enormous prestige of having published a book is almost enough to remove the shame of poor sales. Even a book's rapid disappearance from the shelves does not obscure the fact that the author has at least made an impression on readers.

Erma's column, "At Wit's End," had been running for several years in the early 1960s when Doubleday and Company expressed interest in publishing a compilation of Erma's best columns. For Erma, it was an exciting assignment. She was happily churning out three columns a week for a large number of newspapers, but it would be really something else to produce a book of them!

For the newspaper or magazine writer, seeing one's name on a book is a definite seal of approval—proof that he or she had made the grade, at least in the public eye. Newspaper print was always notoriously short-lived. Erma's mother had been right about the glamour of having a byline in the newspaper: there was none. After all, today's lead story would be wrapped around tomorrow's garbage. Because a humorist was involved in making people laugh rather than in discussing weighty issues of the day, the lifetime of the joke was even more short-lived.

Of course the truth about book sales and the amount of money to be made had not yet reached Erma Bombeck, and she was very happy to collect her columns and have them published in book form. She had already written them. She simply reassembled them in groups under ideas and wrote amusing little subheads to attract the reader who wanted to skim through the works. In order to make the book even more appealing, Doubleday hired an illustrator named Loretta Vollmuth to add line drawings.

The book, titled *At Wit's End,* came out in 1967, and although it did not become an instant best-seller, it did manage to put Erma Bombeck's name on the map. It certainly widened her audience and appreciably broadened her recognition as a writer. And books—even those that do not reach superstar best-selling status—are apt to attract people who frequent their neighborhood libraries. It also helped make Erma Bombeck a name in many rural communities her syndicated column did not reach.

The book tour drove her crazy. People who have not published books cannot imagine the nightmare that is a book tour. She asked herself, What glamour? What glitz? She flew in drafty airplanes, ate beef tips that tasted like wing tips, slept in her underwear while her bags slept in some other city, ironed the next day's clothes on the toilet seat lid, autographed soggy cocktail napkins, and stood at receptions for three hours listening to people tell her they wrote funny letters too and were after her cushy job. She was given microphones that didn't work, she appeared on midnight talk shows where people called in without knowing who she was, and once, a TV makeup man shaved her eyebrows (which, incidentally, never did grow back in). One night she spent three hours in a department store behind a stack of her books. The only exchanges occurred when a woman wanted directions to the rest room and a man came up to ask the price of the desk she was sitting at.

In her recital of the problems and glitches of a book tour, she was putting herself down, having a good laugh at her own expense. But in a way the whole experience was a negative one. She had assumed, as most people do, that publishing a book would lead to instant fame and fortune.

Most people pay no heed to H. L. Mencken's description of a writer as an "ink-stained wretch" (coined when they still used pen and ink to write material). They think only of the rich rewards of writing garnered by a handful of best-selling writers.

Erma Bombeck was not immediately showered with big money. The book sold modestly—probably more than the publishers thought it might—and her royalty checks came in slowly. But the book remained in print throughout Erma's lifetime, bringing in a steady sum each year!

But of course it was a heartbreaker for her at the time. She thought it would be a stepping-stone to a great deal more money than she seemed to be getting. But there were hidden dividends. For instance, publishing a book helped publicize her name on the television talk shows and helped build her name on the lecture circuit, where she had been appearing ever since the column had begun its thrice-a-week incarnation. Contrary to what the public thinks, authors often go on the lecture circuit not to supplement income from the sales of their books but to earn the money they need to live on!

Art Buchwald—no stranger to humor or to Erma Bombeck—recently laughed outright at a talk-show host's assumption that he made his income from his column and his book sales. It was, he said quite succinctly, his *lectures* that made him the money, in some months netting many times the revenue of his efforts in print. Writers of prestigious novels and intellectual tomes have to do the same thing to earn their bread during the off times.

The publication of *At Wit's End,* the book, was successful in the long run for Erma Bombeck. There were very few reviews, but she did become established as a humorist with a national reputation rather than just someone whose picture appeared three times a week in the family newspaper.

"Erma Bombeck is a syndicated columnist who writes humorously of the small, everyday events in the suburban housewife's life," wrote Suzanne Lennon in the *Library Journal*. "In *At Wit's End*, apparently drawn from her columns...she depicts the problems, frustrations and loneliness that afflict many women in this affluent age. Although this subject has been discussed exhaustingly in the last few years, Mrs. Bombeck's flippant, irreverent style, with many clever metaphors and similes, should provide a few chuckles for the harried housewife."

In its "Forecast" section, *Publishers Weekly* had this to say: "Columnist-wife-mother Erma Bombeck describes her book as a 'group therapy session' to cheer up depressed housewives. Mrs. Bombeck humorously re-creates the moments when the kids—or their father—are about to be really too much, the discovery of a figure that isn't what it used to be, intellectual stagnation, recreation, and holiday hysteria...women's club meetings, the children growing up, etc."

According to the publisher, the book did "fairly well," a thinly veiled phrase that meant it was no rocket to the moon, but no out-and-out failure either. The editors at Doubleday wanted another book, but they didn't want just another collection of columns.

They decided to team her up with syndicated cartoonist Bil Keane, creator of "Family Circus." He satirized the middle-class family just as Bombeck did, but from a male point of view. The advantage here would be that Bombeck would be appealing to a male audience as well as a female one. (No one thought that she was appealing much to the men with her first book—although no one really knew. No one knew how many men read her column in the daily newspaper, either.)

Four years after *At Wit's End* was published, the Bombeck-Keane book came out. It had a long title: *Just Wait Til You Have Children of Your Own.* This follow-up book did fairly well, just as the first one had, but it was never a best-seller. It did get a few reviews—more than the first one—but it made little splash in the publishing waters.

The reviewers still didn't have a clear idea of what Erma Bombeck was all about, nor did they know much about the three-times-a-week column she turned out so successfully. A look at two reviews reveals that no one had a handle on her abilities yet.

The *Publishers Weekly* review was on the negative side. "A look at Erma Bombeck, columnist for the *Dayton Journal-Herald,* with illustrations by Bil Keane. This is superficial generation-gap humor that should reassure Middle America. The kids Mrs. Bombeck writes of seem scarcely to be into drugs and politics. What are they into? Orthodontia, phone marathons, unisex dress and hair, sibling rivalry, love affairs in cars, sex education, TV, and rock—although regarding the last, one isn't sure Mrs. Bombeck has touched base, since she calls Joan Baez a rock star. The humor is that of a harassed but gallant suburban parent who may be closer to the old *Saturday Evening Post* covers than to the kids."

The reviewer was searching vainly for some way to assess this material. As a man, he seemed to feel that Erma was behind the times, living a Norman Rockwell life in a postrevolutionary 1970s era. As much as he claimed Erma was out of touch, he himself seemed distanced from the very active suburban life that she was experiencing.

The *Kirkus Service,* an outfit that criticized newly published books for the library buyers, slammed it: "Passably humorous palaver about parents and teenagers—the hair, the telephone, the love life, clothes, the works. Isolated lines have a frayed charm and keep you reading on: 'If the good Lord had meant for you to wear bell-bottoms, he'd have flared your ankles.' But they're few and far between the snappy Roz Russell retorts and the strained banterings. A mini-amusement based on that nonexistent stereotypical kid."

Both reviews missed the point of the real problem with the book—the collaboration was unsuccessful. In fact, the book itself didn't seem to know what it was.

In most humor books, illustrations are used to depict the author's words. Keane's background was mostly in magazine and newspaper cartoons, single-panel jokes in which the funny caption combined with the picture to produce the laugh.

For some reason—possibly it was the way in which Erma Bombeck wrote—the prose and the pictures in the Bombeck-Keane collaboration seemed to be fighting, rather than cooperating, with each other. Erma's writings usually had a narrative with a definite beginning, a middle, and an end. Most of the cartoons were separate sight gags, with original captions.

In order to give some semblance of organization to the book, a group of Keane cartoons, complete with captions, were placed together with one or two Bombeck columns to create a subject: this segment was then given a title like "Sibling Bill of Rights," or "Telephone Fever." Then, because the sections were so short, they were lumped into larger chapterlike segments titled with more gag lines like "How I Discovered I Was Living with a Teenager," "Theories I Have Blown," and "Stone Age Versus Rock Age."

The columns themselves were full-blown Bombeck. The cartoons were perfect Keane. But the way they were assembled somehow seemed to defeat the purpose of their packaging.

Though the results of the collaboration were not encouraging to the editors at Doubleday, they wanted more Erma Bombeck. When her next book came out in 1973, it featured many of her columns, with a few illustrations by an artist named Loretta Krupinski.

The third book had a good gag title: *I Lost Everything in the Post-Natal Depression,* though it had nothing to do with child-bearing or postnatal depression. It was simply a hodgepodge of items she wrote as columns. Some of these columns were expanded, others were cut and joined to other shorter pieces.

Erma was at her best making up gag titles. The book's chapters are perfect examples: "Ironed Sheets Are a Health Hazard," "I Gave Him the Best Year of My Life," "She Has a Cold. Shoot Her," "Put Down Your Brother, You Don't Know Where He's Been," and "We Have Measles...It Must Be Christmas."

"Erma is a spokeswoman for those millions of housebound, children-chasing, food-fixing women who are too busy living and giving to be *someone* or *do something*," the *Library Journal*'s Shirley A. Smith wrote. "In this latest expanded collection of items from her syndicated column 'At Wit's End,' she writes in the tongue-in-cheek style of Jean Kerr and Betty McDonald, giving sometimes insightful, always humorous comments on the current middle-class suburban lifestyle. A truly witty and funny woman; a laugh-till-you-cry book for public libraries."

Publishers Weekly concurred, seeing it as a "housewife's complaint by the popular syndicated women's page columnist who carries wit and hyperbole to the nth degree. Mrs. Bombeck's discernment of the ghastly trivia that drizzle endlessly on the suburban housewife, especially on a loser, is joyous in its precision and rightness. Through thirteen chapters she embroiders the eternal themes: the foibles and fallibilities of hubby; a woman's day—cooking, shopping, bringing up kids, neighbors; marriage in sickness and health; Christmas shopping.... The woman who'll buy this book knows nothing's a non sequitur when everything leads to something else."

Pamela Marsh wrote in the *Christian Science Monitor*, "This is no Class A Number 1 out-of-control housewife we have here, but a deliberate comic who doesn't place a foot or a word wrong without deliberate intent."

Doubleday was happy enough with the book to order a first printing of 70,000, quite large for the average humor book. But Erma Bombeck's audience was growing.

At about the time she began putting together collections of columns for her books, the Bombecks had moved from their home in Centerville, Ohio, to a thirty-acre farm in Bellbrook, Ohio. They expected it to be the last move they would make. The kids would be educated nearby, and Bill would not need to change jobs.

At first, the bucolic background enchanted Erma. The thirty acres that surrounded them cut them off from any loud neighbors. In addition, the isolation allowed Erma to relax as never before.

The kids thought a bit differently. They felt that since this was obviously an old farmhouse, there should be farm animals around. None of them, of course, knew anything about farm animals, nor did they make a move to acquire any. Furthermore, there were many repairs to be made on the house, which was far from new. Erma was traveling quite a bit now, pushing her books and speaking on television, and she was not always in the house. But the others were. And she could sense the complaints, and hear them voiced aloud as well. Somehow the idea of being gentlemen farmpersons—or whatever they took themselves to be—did not seem to be working out.

Erma gave a speech one night in Phoenix, Arizona. Her lecture circuit work was improving, and she had the audience eating out of her hand. But in turn, Phoenix had Erma eating out of its hand. There was an absolutely marvelous atmosphere about the place. The big sky. The spectacular sunrises and sunsets. The rugged mountains. The desert cactus on the horizon.

Erma could not forget that night, nor could she forget Phoenix. Within months, the Bombeck family moved out of the farmhouse in Ohio and made their way down to Arizona to resettle. It was a joyous trip.

Bill Bombeck immediately got a job as a high school principal in Phoenix and reveled in the work. Erma continued publicizing her books, which was her main occupation, and visited scores of towns all over America to talk about herself and amuse her audiences.

In the back of her mind Erma knew it was a crucial time in her career. She had to try something *new*. And she had a pretty good idea of what it would be.

CHAPTER EIGHT

❧

The Story of Suburbia

Erma Bombeck was by now a very successful syndicated newspaper columnist. She had also been doing a regular monthly column, which ran from 1969 to 1975 for the magazine *Good Housekeeping*. In addition, she had been selling various scribblings to other women's magazines; these articles appeared sporadically. And she had put together three books, each of which had enjoyed certain degrees of success in the bookstores.

But she wanted more. She knew her strength was not factual material but fictional material. She wanted to write a *story* of suburbia—a story long enough to be published as a novel. She talked this over with her publisher, Doubleday and Company, but apparently there was not enough interest to give her a go-ahead. Because of the ongoing success of her three books, they thought it would be best to stick to the usual format, rather than try something that might frighten off readers who were fans of the material she used in her thrice-weekly columns. And so they passed on it.

There was a salesman at Doubleday named Aaron Priest who had always been a fan of Erma Bombeck's. He even thought she could write a bestseller if she worked it right—and he told her so. When Doubleday turned down Erma's new idea, she thought of Aaron Priest, and telephoned him. Priest was confident that Erma could pull off what she intended to do—write a book that was a kind of tongue-in-cheek look at suburbia, paralleling it to the settling of the West. He told her to send him some sample pages of the book and a good punchy outline, and he'd send it around.

When he received her outline, he telephoned her immediately. "This could be it," he said in words bursting with confidence. And, indeed, within two weeks, he sold the book, *The Grass Is Always Greener over the Septic Tank,* to McGraw-Hill. He pitched Doubleday first, but they turned him down because they thought the price he was asking was too high. McGraw-Hill didn't think so at all.

By now Aaron Priest had become Erma Bombeck's agent. He confessed that when he was pushing her books as a salesman for Doubleday, he had never realized what a pittance she was getting for writing them. He was confident that things would work out very well this time around.

Erma was given a year in which to finish the book. And she took it. She was a very busy woman with three columns a week and a novel to write! But she loved the challenge.

Later on, in a humorous dialogue with Judy Klemesrud of *The New York Times* after the book was published, Erma revealed that she had been inspired to write it after reading James A. Michener's best-seller *Centennial,* a novel about the settling of the West. "I really thought suburbia was the last great frontier," she said, tongue firmly in cheek. "I thought about how people got into their station wagons and shouted, 'Station wagons, ho!' Of course I didn't go as far back in history as Michener did—I just went back to the Welcome Wagon lady."

Bombeck worked hard on this book. "I'm a very disciplined writer," she explained. "When I do a book I work seven days a week from 8:30 A.M. to 3:30 in the afternoon." And she worked on her column at the same time.

But there was even more in the works for her. In a world entirely different from book publishing—the television industry—there were movements that promised either great new things or imminent disaster. For years, NBC had reigned as top dog in the morning hours. The *Today Show* was the show for anyone pushing a book, any celebrity who needed exposure, any star who wanted to hype his latest epic.

The brass at ABC-TV decided to do something about it. Several of the movers and shakers at ABC believed that NBC's show had become somewhat stodgy and a little too serious for the people who wanted to get up, have a quick look at the news, and then maybe sit around and have a cup of coffee while listening to interesting people.

Tom Brokaw and Jane Pauley served as *Today*'s anchors, and they were considered by many viewers to be somewhat remote, aloof, and even dull by some standards. Of course, *Today* also had Willard Scott, their countryboy gofer who came on for amusing little bits here and there. But, generally, the atmosphere was serious. According to the ABC brass, it plodded.

ABC wanted to open up the humor a bit. In other words, come on with a bang, get the horror news over, wrap up the killings, and then get to some amusing celebrity interviews or comedy routines.

Bob Shanks was assigned to produce the new show. Shanks assembled a very impressive slate of people, including David Hartman, who had acted in a TV Western called *Lucas Tanner;* Nancy Dussalt, a TV actress; Jack Anderson, a syndicated political newspaper columnist; Rona Barrett, whose beat was Hollywood; Jonathan Winters, a roly-poly, very funny, offbeat comedian; and Geraldo Rivera.

Shanks knew that the majority of people who might choose to sit around after the news ended to listen to celebrities and hotshots schmooze on morning television were housewives—and he wanted someone who could appeal directly to them. And of course he thought almost immediately of Erma Bombeck.

She had appeared on a number of talk shows to push her three books; she had been on the *Tonight Show,* the evening companion of the *Today Show;* she had appeared on Phil Donahue's show, and a lot of other local stations all over the country. Shanks liked what he saw.

When Shanks approached Erma, she was reluctant—not because she was afraid to accept a new challenge, but because she was afraid she would have to appear live in New York with David Hartman and Nancy Dussalt. That would simply be too much for her. And indeed Shanks wanted that if at all possible. It meant that she could be worked in at the last moment if the schedule became disordered or an extra filler was needed.

Shanks wanted a two- or three-minute "bit" two mornings a week for his new show, which would be called *Good Morning America.* In the end, Shanks capitulated and agreed to let Erma film her bits in Phoenix at the ABC outlet there. When that detail was ironed out to her satisfaction, Erma agreed to take the job and immediately started to think up "bits" for her role.

It was a good decision for Erma. She had appeared on enough television shows to feel at ease in front of the camera. And she had worked out a way to make her remarks seem a bit livelier than they had been when she was just breaking into the business.

And so, in 1975, *Good Morning America* hit the ground running, and the difference between it and the *Today Show* was evident from the beginning. The set was a stylized suburban home complete with living room and kitchen, where news could be read or Julia Child could share recipes with the viewers. *Today* still had its anchors seated behind a solid nineteenth-century desk before a backdrop of the Manhattan skyline.

David Hartman's easygoing, all-American boy personality made the biggest difference. The years he spent acting in Westerns had helped mold him into the laconic, silent cowboy hero modeled after Gary Cooper. From the beginning, levity, not seriousness, characterized the atmosphere of *Good Morning America*.

Though a number of the projected regulars were dropped quickly, others survived. Erma was good—or maybe she was just lucky. She survived. She was reviewed by television critics, some of them enthusiastic and some downright hostile. Nevertheless, most of them approved of her presence on the *Good Morning America* show. She fit into the format as devised by Bob Shanks, and she worked in well with David Hartman, even though the two of them were never face to face on the set.

"Erma Bombeck was funny enough in her housewife as humorist role, which may be rewarding if some real housewives get a high out of it," said the *Baltimore Sun*.

Though the *St. Louis Globe-Democrat* didn't focus specifically on Erma, it was generally critical of the show. "The laugh track accompanying Erma Bombeck's commentary wasn't needed. Phony laughs are bad enough on prime-time comedies. At that hour of the morning, they are sickening."

C. W. Skipper of the *Houston Post* said Erma was "a very funny woman." "I'd be happy just to sit there and chuckle when Bombeck is on, but ABC has seen fit to give her what I'm sure is a laugh track in hopes of stimulating laughter. Or else she has a small audience of friends and neighbors who seem to laugh on cue.

"Bombeck also seems used to working without editors, and I don't believe ABC has given her one. I don't think some sentences came out exactly as she intended.

"One came out this way: 'How can I keep a bathroom clean with children?' What she intended to say was something like, 'If I have children around the house, how can I keep a bathroom clean?'" A quibble, certainly.

The *Washington Star-News* wrote off the *Good Morning America* show as a "kind of low-brow *Reader's Digest*." It liked Erma's "sharply focused routine" but hated the "canned laughter," which prompted the viewer to wonder how all those people got into her living room in the first place. But the routine caught on, the canned laughter was dumped within weeks, and the segment was vastly improved.

In adapting her material from the page to television, Erma varied her style of comedy very little. A script for a two-and-a-half-minute bit was shorter than an ordinary daily print strip. But the material and the way it was handled were the same. Some of her appearances on television seemed to be simple readings of her columns, as indeed they were intended to be.

She did occasionally change her routine and try for a more visual type of humor. She once interviewed a hog at a farm that was using hogs to research diet patterns in human beings. She traveled to the hog fair, discussed the situation with a scientist there, and then held a gag interview with one of the experimental hogs.

In another segment, she performed an entire skit without any words except for the initial introduction. "They say girls are neater than boys," she said. Then she performed the rest of the segment in pantomime, showing the fallacy of the cliché. The camera carefully examined each piece of junk as she pulled it out from under her daughter's bed, from behind the dresser, under the blankets, and so on.

Erma usually delivered her monologue directly to the camera. Dressed as a typical suburban housewife, she discoursed on blenders, automobile jargon, jogging, and the daily trials of suburban life. Occasionally she would slip in a serious piece. Before Christmas one year, she performed a piece about how, without young children around, Christmas was more sad than happy.

Not all reviewers were enamored of Erma Bombeck's appearances on the *Good Morning America* show. *Time* magazine critic Frank Rich wrote in 1978 that her appearances were "one of the most depressing spectacles on television." He continued, "She delivers her one-liners in a strident vibrato; she luxuriates in canned laughter as though it were the praise of a Nobel Prize jury." He concluded, "Bombeck used to satirize the vulgarity of American suburbia; now she epitomizes it."

Erma's segment on ABC-TV's *Good Morning America* lasted for eleven years. She eventually quit the show because she felt she was getting to the point where she could plead overwork.

Erma continued to work on her "novel" about

suburbia during her first year on TV. Her original title for the completed book was *As the Tupperware Turns,* but, as she told an interviewer, the Tupperware people got upset. "Then we thought about *Confessions of a Girl Scout Cookie Pusher,* but the Girl Scouts didn't like that. Then it came upon me that the septic tank people aren't militant, and so that was it."

The title was *The Grass Is Always Greener over the Septic Tank.* "The characters are based on people I used to know," she said, "and the town is based on Centerville, Ohio, where I used to live."

Someone once asked her if the title of the book was a truism—that is, *is* the grass always greener over the septic tank? "It sure is," Erma said. "Moisture and goodies come up through the soil. One woman told me she even started the plants in her garden over the septic tank. I told her I'd never eat a salad at her house."

The book appeared in 1976—about a year or so after Erma had begun her TV appearances. The novel was a vast improvement over her first three collections of columns. A narrative thread, however tenuous, held the material together and gave it a semiconventional story line. But the real advance was in her writing style and in the tone and the feeling of the characters.

This satire of suburban life was much more penetrating and evocative than her column humor. The usual problems, minuscule bothers such as crabgrass, high taxes, and teenagers, were well covered, but bigger issues appeared as well, including the monotony of suburbia, the uniformity of life among its residents, the restrictions on individuality, and the unwavering focus on social status and money.

"She manages with the deftness of a trapeze artist to come up with a smile on her face in the midst of unaccountable maneuvers," wrote H. T. Andrews of *Best Sellers* in January 1976. "She takes her joy and strength from the things she satirizes—we need more of that!"

Not all the reviews were positive, however. *Library Journal*, which had always applauded her books, suddenly turned against her. "Bombeck's humor is aimed at pointing up the absurdities of the suburban American, middle-class lifestyle, with its timing; its real and imagined 'necessities,'" wrote J. W. Powell, who went on to complain that the author's humor had become diluted by overexposure in newspapers and on television.

Ms. magazine's Jane Holtz Kay wrote, "Erma Bombeck is not alone. She is out there where everybody's been headed this last quarter century: she is out there spinning her wheels in the greatest migration in American history. Or, to put it as she does in this tale of her pioneer days, Erma is at the garage so often she has her own key to the rest room. She is 'U-Haul Mother of the Year.'…

"Shallow stuff? Oppressively cheerful? Maybe so. Still, she sees it all…the skirmishes and the 'Major Battles Fought in the Suburbs,' the plastic rush, the franchise freak-out, the land-use patterns that made for a nation of obsessive lawn-keepers…. Erma Bombeck, student of the Suckerware set (as she calls it), is a big-time writer and no stay-at-home. Still that makes her sense that the suburban septic, or antiseptic, way of life is on the wane all the more noteworthy."

Frederick H. Guidry, book editor of the *Christian Science Monitor*, viewed it this way: "Exaggeration—sometimes gross—is…one of Bombeck's specialties. When she is negotiating for a washer repairman, she tries to impress the office with her desperation. 'Desperate is sending your kids to school in under-wear made from broiler foil. Desperate is washing sheets in a double boiler. Don't you understand? I need a repairman.'

"Bombeck also leads her readers through such

slow-motion agonies as parking the Winnebago trailer ('There's an Airstream coming in at four o'clock,' an aviation-minded bystander warns)... [She knows] better than to try to solve today's problems. With skillful satire, [she] is mining national worries for rueful, golden laughter."

The Grass Is Always Greener over the Septic Tank was published in 1976, and when it appeared, Erma Bombeck hit the big time. There were good reasons for the huge success of *Grass*. First, it was an original work by Erma, not a collection of her past columns. Second, it got marvelous publicity from the fact that Erma had been toiling steadily on *Good Morning America* before the book was released. The combined exposure boosted book sales. The reviews helped too, although they were not all raves. In the end, *Grass* was an unmitigated success.

But what could she do now to top it?

CHAPTER NINE

Working in the Pits

With things finally beginning to fall into place for Erma Bombeck—on television and on the printed page—she had become what Hollywood loves to call "hot property." Now movie moguls began hovering around this new discovery, trying to think up ways *they* could profit from her talent and energy. It didn't take long before some of the hotshots at ABC-TV suggested that Erma adapt *The Grass Is Always Greener over the Septic Tank* as a made-for-television movie.

Erma was certainly willing, but she knew her limitations. She had to write her regular column three times a week, and she had to appear on ABC twice a week. That in itself was a whole working week. She simply could not squeeze in the time to adapt her own work, much as she would have liked to take a shot at it. She was unfamiliar with adapting novels for TV, and she held back, bowing out of the offer. However, she was open to having someone else adapt her work.

It often happens that as one "in" celebrity is fading from view, another "in" celebrity appears on the horizon. As Erma's star rose, the star of Carol Burnett—whose prime-time television show had finally come to the end of its long run—was beginning to fade just a bit. But Erma and Carol Burnett were both comedians, regardless of their other talents and abilities.

And so Carol Burnett was selected to star in the film version of *Grass*. She was teamed with Charles Grodin to play the newlyweds trying to make it in suburbia. The cast also included Linda Gray (a big hit on TV's soap opera *Dallas*), Alex Rocco, Vicki Belmonte, and Robert Sampson. Robert Day would direct.

Dick Clair and Jenna McMahon, two Emmy Award-winning TV writers, were hired to write the script. They produced a scenario that would need to be changed only slightly to serve as a pilot for a weekly television series. The big money was in series television, not in movies, and ABC was hoping to make the movie into a series.

The show was finally broadcast on October 23, 1978, two years after the publication of the book. It was not greeted with universal acclaim. In fact, the consensus even among Erma Bombeck's friends was that it was a pretty poor example of a suburban comedy. There were both good and bad elements. One of the good elements was Carol Burnett, and some of the reviewers praised her for her work.

A reviewer from St. Petersburg tried to interview Erma by telephone before the show was aired. But she was too busy at the time to talk to him. "I had to settle for watching a preview of the movie," he wrote later in the *St. Petersburg Times.* "I crawled back to the office doubled up in laughter. Nobody better articulates the American woman than Erma Bombeck."

He explained that the show was an adaptation of a novel about a city family that moved to the suburbs. "The movie sticks relatively close to Mrs. Bombeck's book of the same name." Noting that she did not write the script but that it was assigned to two other writers, he said, "They did a fine job of creating continuity from Mrs. Bombeck's one-liner jokes."

Carol Burnett, he said, "is at her best." "There are some truthfully humorous sketches within the movie on being visited by an insurance salesman, having a house party, and spraying the dog for fleas."

But his was one of the few positive reviews. Many more shared the opinion of Frank Rich of *Time* magazine, who had earlier lambasted the book. In his review of the movie, he generally attacked Erma rather than Carol Burnett. The best thing about the movie, he said, was that Erma Bombeck herself did not play the heroine. "That odious chore has fallen instead to Carol Burnett, an actress who is often capable of extracting humor from even the most puerile material. This is one of her rare failures...Bombeck's stale jokes about crabgrass and Tupperware parties defy levitation: the cutesie plot is predictable to anyone who has ever encountered any incarnation of *Please Don't Eat the Daisies*."

Rich also pointed out that the director, Robert Day, did not give much direction to Carol Burnett or the other cast members. Day's concept of great dramatic intensity, he said, was to wind up a scene with a close-up of characters rising from a couch. However, Rich did admit that one player was consciously animated while on the screen—Charles Grodin. Rich contended that Grodin was simply rushing about exploring the set for some way to escape the surroundings "in a quite understandable state of panic."

It's unlikely that Erma even read this review, for in 1979 her attention was focused elsewhere: Bill Bombeck finally realized his dream to run the Boston Marathon. In the beginning, Erma admitted that she had never really understood why he wanted to do it, but she realized that it was something that he sincerely wanted to do, and she helped prepare him for the event.

In preparation, he would rise early every morning and begin jogging to loosen up. Then he would perform a number of stretching exercises to get his body ready for the ordeal. He had had his physicals, and his doctor had told him he could do it, but Erma was worried. She knew that sometimes your body simply wouldn't answer your demands. But she helped him as best she could.

The day finally arrived, and the Bombecks were both on the scene in Boston. It seemed to Erma that Bill Bombeck was lost in the mass of cheering people. He ran the course in three hours and twenty-two minutes, a fairly respectable time! It was a great success for Bill Bombeck.

The bad publicity surrounding the poor reception of the made-for-TV film *Grass* did not really spill over onto Erma Bombeck partly because her fifth book had just hit the stands. As soon as Erma had finished writing *Grass,* she began another, tentatively titled *Life Is a Parade, and I'm Standing behind Bill Russell.* The finished book, *If Life Is a Bowl of Cherries, What Am I Doing in the Pits?* was greeted with much fanfare.

On the strength of her success with the best-seller *Grass,* she was beginning to get the treatment usually reserved for showbiz personalities. In January 1978, *Newsweek* ran a one-page piece about her titled "The $500,000 Housewife." After extolling the merits of *Grass*—500,000 copies sold in hardcover—Diane K. Shah revealed that paperback rights to *Pits* had just been sold for a whopping million dollars. According to the story, Erma uttered a typical Bombeckism when asked how she celebrated the event: "I didn't do my laundry for three days."

Erma Bombeck was on a public relations roll. Her name was appearing everywhere that it counted—and some places that it didn't. People were paying attention to her. In 1978, stories about Erma Bombeck saturated the media.

In February, *Ladies' Home Journal* ran a special feature by Bombeck on women's rights. It was not a humor column, but a stronger article on feminism.

In April, *Good Housekeeping,* for which she had once done a regular monthly column, assigned Phyllis Battelle to profile her for the magazine.

At *The New York Times Book Review,* Herbert Mitgang was assigned to run a story on Erma Bombeck's newest book when it appeared in April.

In May, *People* magazine did a treatment on Bombeck, casting it as a question-and-answer interview. The article reported that *Pits* had already "vaulted to No. 2 in its second week on the bestseller list." Asked if she felt at all like a television celebrity—which by then, of course, she was—Bombeck responded, "No. I'm a one-woman show. I do my own makeup. I sweep up and vacuum. But for someone who was never recognized by her butcher when she got the next number, this is a really big thing for me. I never get over the shock of someone recognizing me."

In September, Martin L. Gross tape-recorded an interview with Erma, a seven-page transcript of which ran in *Book Digest.*

Writing her successful syndicated column, "At Wit's End," in 1975.

Juggling three children and three columns a week.

(Photofest)

Erma as she appeared on "Good Morning America" in 1976.　*(Photofest)*

Swapping stories with John Willis, co-host of "Good Day!"
(Photofest)

Never without a smile.
*(Ron Frehm,
AP/Wide World Photos)*

Erma congratulates her husband, Bill, after he completes the Phoenix Marathon in 1982.

(Seidel, AP/Wide World Photos)

Chatting about her new TV show, "Maggie," with Gary Collins on "Hour Magazine." *(Photofest)*

In keeping with the parade's theme, "A Celebration of Laughter," Erma keeps the crowd in stitches at the 1985 Tournament of Roses Parade in Pasadena, California.

(Lacy Atkins, AP/Wide World Photos)

Erma waves from the car as the Grand Marshal of the Rose Bowl Parade. *(Reed Saxon, AP/Wide World Photos)*

Always a favorite guest on "The Tonight Show."

(Suzie Bleeden, Globe Photos)

Erma with her husband, Bill, her daughter, Betsy, and her two sons, Andy and Matthew.

(Douglas Kirkland, Sygma)

Erma looks on as Representative Pat Schroeder is caught making rabbit ears behind talk show host Phil Donahue at the 25th Anniversary of "The Donahue Show."

(Bob Strong, AP/ Wide World Photos)

Caught in a light moment.

(Douglas Kirkland, Sygma)

Relaxing at home.

(Rona Kasen, Globe Photos)

In October, *Ladies' Home Journal* ran an excerpt from a book called *Beginnings,* by Thomas C. Hunter, in which Erma Bombeck's story, "How I Made It to the Top," was featured.

This attention helped keep *Pits* on the best-seller list. In addition, Erma was everywhere on the talk shows hyping the book.

The reviews of *Pits* began to appear in April, and they were fairly good. Even the sophisticated *New York Times* featured a review. An editor of the *Times Book Review* and one-time author, Richard R. Lingeman, gave her a fairly balanced review.

"Her style is a bit hectic and slapdash, sounding as though she scrawled the column on the back of a laundry list while stirring the evening's Hamburger Helper," Lingeman wrote. "It's the kind of style that is a half beat ahead of her readers, giving them a twitch of recognition and the feeling 'I might have written that myself.'"

Lingeman concluded, "So one is left admiring Mrs. Bombeck for giving voice to a segment of the population that is not always heard from, but the trivia of whose lives may be, on the higher scale of things, as significant as anything that takes place in the male or sophisticated or urbane world. There is truth in the best of her humor as well as sanity;

what it lacks is the lift and play of language and wit. Sometimes she serves up a meat loaf extended with empty gags; even home cooking can pall, if not relieved by the occasional soufflé."

Other critics were much kinder. "In her syndicated column, Bombeck likes to picture herself as a frowzy, inept, frustrated, catastrophe-prone housewife," wrote *Publishers Weekly.* "She is, of course, a sharp and very funny lady, and her latest collection of sketches is generally right on target.... In this collection, Bombeck casts a merrily jaundiced eye on the seventies scene, advising the reader how to survive the tennis craze, to detect a spurious picture of glamorous career women who double as super hausfraus, to cope with the thought of premium offspring living in coed dorms. She is less successful when she waxes sentimental—several sketches verge on the maudlin. But her satirized description of family relationships will probably captivate the same audience that enjoyed *The Grass Is Always Greener over the Septic Tank.*"

Art Buchwald, a close friend of Erma Bombeck's from the early days of her writing career, wrote, "Before I get down to the business of reviewing Erma Bombeck's latest book, I think I have to make one thing perfectly clear: I know the author personally.

We even had a little thing going between us at a Holiday Inn on the outskirts of Gary, Indiana, several years ago when we were both reading *Passages* and having our midlife crises at the same time."

Buchwald described Erma just as he saw her. "Despite what you see on television, which distorts the human face and figure, Erma is a tall, long-legged, beautiful natural blonde with Ivory soap skin, ruby-red pouting lips, Maidenform body, a waist that could easily belong to Alicia Markova, and hands that have never touched dishwater."

After comparing her to Elizabeth Taylor, Julie Andrews, Rita Hayworth, and Princess Grace of Monaco, Buchwald went on, "For years Erma Bombeck was thought of as nothing but a sex object." Then she suddenly started writing a humor column, and "people realized there was a lot more to Erma Bombeck than being a poster in every Air Force ready room, every college dormitory, and every foxhole in the First Marine Division."

What happened? The inevitable. "She became the Betty Friedan of the Women's Humor Movement. Now, little girls all over America, when asked what they want to be when they grow up, reply 'Erma Bombeck.'"

Following that introduction, Buchwald wrote, "In

this book, Erma gives us a sampling of her work. The trick is to see if you can read a paragraph without laughing out loud. I can't, and I don't laugh easily, particularly when I'm reading a competitor who is taking food out of my children's mouths."

Erma Bombeck was riding a wave like an expert surfer. *The Grass Is Always Greener over the Septic Tank* sold 500,000 copies in hardcover. A year and a half later, *If Life Is a Bowl of Cherries, What Am I Doing in the Pits?* raised Erma's best-seller status to 700,000 hardcover copies.

But she wasn't resting on those laurels. She was still turning out books—along with her three weekly columns and her appearances on *Good Morning America.* In 1979 she published *Aunt Erma's Cope Book,* a satire of self-help books, which sold nearly 600,000 copies. In *Aunt Erma's Cope Book,* Erma invented a story line in which she, a self-proclaimed "perfect woman," made an exploratory tour through sixty-two self-help books, sampling all kinds of fads and ploys to try to understand and improve herself. She wrote "After reading sixty-two books and articles on how to deal with oneself, I realized something was missing. A sense of humor.

I cannot believe that people look into the mirror that reflects their actions and behavior and keep a straight face." Erma's satire did very well in the bookstores, and even received a number of good reviews.

Caroline Seebohm in *The New York Times Book Review* wrote, "In each chapter [Bombeck] exposes herself to the various home therapies (Sensual Needlepoint, Inner Jogging, Color-Coding Your Leftovers) promoted in such catchily titled books as *The Sub-Total Woman....* But of course our Erma doesn't get self-improved at all, and at the end finds her biorhythms still out of sync. When she gives up on the literature of self-help, she suffers withdrawal symptoms: sweaty palms and dry throat. These are good jokes. There are some less good jokes in passages (or packages) of dialogue and anecdotes that permit transitions between the good jokes. It's all very light indeed and you can read it in one sitting, while you wait for your waxy yellow buildup to dry."

"Few contemporary humorists are more popular or prolific than housewife, mother, and nationally syndicated columnist Erma Bombeck," wrote Dennis Petticoffer, in the *Library Journal*. "*Aunt Erma's Cope*

Book satirizes self-help advocates and so-called friends whose candor and concern provoke them to hand out free advice. Inevitably their tips turn out to be more burdening than helpful…. Bolstered by an underlying 'be thyself' philosophy and the 'medicine of laughter,' Erma's tortured (tongue-in-cheek) testimonials may actually be more therapeutic than most serious self-help books. The lighthearted volume is sure to be in demand."

Leslie Riley Cannon's review in the *Cincinnati Enquirer* said, "Erma Bombeck is an important national resource, like coal and soft toilet paper. One day her face will be on a stamp—under the heading 'Humorist, author, and think-thin activist.' Until the day when she gets the serious recognition she deserves, it's up to her readers to give her the recognition she has earned."

The *Los Angeles Herald Examiner*'s Carol A. Crotts wrote, "First a word about Erma Bombeck. Not enough can be said about this woman. A poet laureate of suburbia, she single-handedly has brought to the dumped-upon states of housewifery and motherhood what they need most—perspective, which is to say, a realization of *commedia dell'arte*. For that alone, she deserves sainthood."

Even if she had once felt that she was standing behind Bill Russell in the parade of life, Erma Bombeck was now standing tall on her own, and she had become a household name after the successes of her fourth, fifth, and sixth books.

CHAPTER TEN

~

The Political Erma

In 1972, Congress approved a constitutional amendment guaranteeing equal rights for women. The amendment stated, "Equality of rights under the law shall not be denied or abridged by the United States or any state on account of sex," and "that Congress shall have the power to enforce by appropriate legislation the provisions of this article."

Once approved by Congress, an amendment to the Constitution must be ratified by three-fourths of the states (thirty-eight of them) within ten years before becoming law. Within a year of its Senate approval, the ERA was ratified by thirty states.

Even though it was obvious that most Americans favored the amendment, the ERA slowly became one of the most divisive issues of the time.

Although it was generally against her nature to participate in any kind of political action, Erma Bombeck became involved in the debate. No comedian can be "on" all the time, making jokes and keeping her fans perpetually in stitches. Even Erma Bombeck exercised a more serious, more personal, more subdued side. That was the side that convinced her to support the ERA in a very public way.

"People write me and say, 'Gee, you could do so much good if you'd write about such and such.'" But, she said, "I couldn't do any good at all because I'd lose my audience. I don't have a message. I write to make myself feel better. I started the column out of sheer boredom, and one reason my column is read is that people want relief from the grimness they find in the rest of the paper. They want to laugh at something."

She had made that statement in 1971, the year before the ERA was approved by Congress. She still wanted to be known as a columnist who never made pronouncements on "anything more controversial than static cling," as *People* magazine put it.

When she started her column, she confined herself strictly to ironing boards, kids, husbands, and household situations. She was also suspicious of activists, political and social, and people with agendas. Actually, they were excellent targets for her satirical thrusts. She once called hard-core women's liberationists "roller derby dropouts and Russian pole-vaulting types."

But a great deal had happened to the American housewife, her greatest supporter, since she started writing. The housewife for whom she wrote when she started had changed as much as she had over the years between World War II and the ERA.

"I'm writing for a different woman now," she pointed out. "She's not standing behind the picture window anymore. She's taken the bus and gone into town. My life has been changed by the same things that have changed all women. My horizons are broader—not just kids, tuna recipes, and crabgrass—and so are the readers' horizons."

Erma Bombeck preferred "playing it down the middle" to becoming an active feminist. She supported the Equal Rights Amendment, but she did not belong to the National Organization for Women. She resented the fact that the leaders of the women's liberation movement never sought to enlist the services of the housewife in their battle for equality.

She would always remember her first impression of Betty Friedan, a leader in the fight for women's rights. "When Betty Friedan came to our town in the mid-sixties and spoke, we roared when she made some comments about how come [television] commercials put women down—captains in the toilet tank and that sort of thing. Friedan was furious when we laughed. 'This isn't funny,' she shouted. 'This is serious.' Of course, it was funny to us housewives. The problem with the women's movement is that it's been too elitist." Erma meant that the leaders of the movement had usually been women who had never been housewives, had never had children, and, in some cases, had never even been married.

Erma went on, "One day in a leading magazine I saw a story called 'Today's Woman on the Go.' At the top of the article was a picture of a well-stacked blonde at a construction site with a group of men around her while she read blueprints to them. I noted her shoes were coordinated with her Gucci yellow hard hat. The second picture showed her in a pair of flowing pajamas standing over a stove stirring her filet-mignon helper (recipe on page 36) while her husband tossed the salad and her children lovingly set the table. It made me want to spit up."

Erma believed in the women's liberation movement, but she voiced her complaints about its methods: "They picked out the American housewife as the battleground for the whole movement, but they didn't invite us to the war. I would personally like to wring the neck of whoever invented that phrase 'just a housewife' because, basically, that's what I still am."

In addition, Bombeck noted, "No one ever asked me to make a stand. Which I think is fairly typical. We housewives were the last to be asked what we wanted. That's probably why the amendment is in trouble today. Finally the feminists are coming to us and saying, 'We can't do it without you.'"

But, she asked, "When did a woman selling orange slices in a dime store become more impressive than a woman who did a darned good job raising three kids for twenty years?"

Though she deliberately avoided controversy in her columns, she discovered that, over the years, it had become much more difficult to keep the column clean. She began tackling more serious subjects, but she tried to keep her writing free of anything that she wouldn't want her own children to read. "I am antiabortion. But I don't want to inflict my beliefs on other people. I'll do it privately, but I won't do it in a column. I'll inflict my kids, my husband, my marriage, my home, domestic situations—anything I think is going to make them laugh that day. But not serious things. [These things are] not for the columns or the books. Lots of subjects can't be handled humorously. I stick close to home—I'm still exploiting my children, husband, and family life. I know where my domain is."

But she didn't stick close to home physically. She traveled hundreds of miles on speaking tours in favor of ERA ratification before the movement died in 1982. She also worked to solicit local support for battered wives and children in Arizona. And she served on the boards of the Arizona Kidney Foundation and other local groups.

She did change her attitude in a number of areas. "I've undergone a transition. I'm into new things. I'm writing from a different vantage point now, not dealing with motherhood constantly. The status of women has broadened my horizons. It's been great for me."

In 1978, she began touring the United States speaking in favor of the Equal Rights Amendment. By January 1979, she and Liz Carpenter, a Texas Democrat and former press secretary for Lady Bird Johnson, were in North Carolina trying to persuade voters to ratify the ERA. She played nice girl to Carpenter's tough girl in their joint appearances, lightening her serious points with jokes. She once described herself as a "nice girl out of the utility room who is used to sorting socks." She told her listeners that they had nothing to fear from the ERA.

In Iowa during the late spring of 1980, the dynamic duo were once again paired off in the nice girl/tough girl approach. Her speech parodied the presidential campaign, satirizing Ronald Reagan, Jimmy Carter, and John Anderson.

"This is the Bombeck-Carpenter initial Presidential Fundraiser and Tupperware Party," she said, to rally the troops. "We believe the country is ready for a woman in the White House who doesn't do windows or floors." She continued in a light vein, explaining with tongue in cheek the platform they had approved, and the catchphrases they had written in order to get press coverage and encourage protest marches.

"We favor a child on every pot."

"You have nothing to fear but cellulite."

"Has Ronald Reagan ever gone into maternity clothes at two weeks? Has Jimmy Carter ever lusted for an after-five dress and gotten a flannel nightgown? Has John Anderson ever taken a knot out of a shoestring with his teeth that a kid has wet on all day long?"

She also noted that the typical housewife did not exist anymore—if she ever had existed. The increase in the number of working mothers, she said, now allowed her to change her jokes to reflect the difference. For example, now she could write about a child who telephoned, dragging his mother out of a high-level business conference to ask her whether or not he could share a bottle of Diet Pepsi with his brother. Or, she could write about a child who called up to announce he had been in a fight, was bleeding, and was lying on a sofa that no one had as yet Scotchgarded; what should he do?

But, she pointed out, even though she believed in the ERA and traveled the country to promote it, she felt that her column was not the place to bring up the issue. "They are two separate things," she explained. The ERA, she believed, was a good thing for the country because the United States was "founded on compassionate laws for everyone."

Earlier during Jimmy Carter's administration (he served as president from 1977 to 1981) Erma Bombeck had been appointed to be a member of the President's Advisory Committee for Women. In public, she tended to minimize her importance on the committee. "Really," she told a reporter, "I'm picked for the public appearance and show-business part of things."

But she was in good company, though she downplayed her own credentials. Lena Epps Brooker, Suzanne Monson, Mayor Isabella Cannon, and Lynda Bird Robb were all members. Unfortunately, the committee had a sad history. Soon after its inception, it was torn apart when the president dismissed its first chairperson, Bella S. Abzug. Twenty-five of the forty committee members resigned. Erma was one of the fifteen who remained. Those who resigned felt that the committee had lost its effectiveness because of negative publicity it had received.

Erma, however, was praised for her work on the committee. "Bombeck is too shy to admit that she's the one who told the committee to concentrate on the ERA," said Esther Landa, former head of the National Council of Jewish Women. "When she has something to say, people listen."

Erma once told *The New York Times* that she attended the committee meetings because she got a better insight into women and could see the frustration boiling up inside them. "That's what I wrote about, frustration." She had another reason for working on the committee. "I'm doing it for my kids. It will be important to them. It's also a great feeling to be part of history. I wish that they could get this on my tombstone: "She got Missouri for the ERA.""

Other supporters of the Equal Rights Amendment usually fell back on political rhetoric to persuade people to support the proposition. Erma did not. She relied, as always, on her quick wit and snappy responses.

Occasionally, during her travels for the ERA, a fan would approach her before the speech, saying, "I hope you're not going to disappoint me, Erma," to which she would reply, "I hope I'm not." She felt a great responsibility to her readers, and deeply believed that the amendment would positively impact women's lives.

No fans were disappointed in her. They rallied behind her. She changed plenty of opinions with her humor and her unique approach to the politics of ERA. Women came to call her a "voice of sanity"—a contrast to the shrill cries of the other advocates.

She had her detractors as well. The lieutenant governor of a Southern state said that she should be home having babies. "My babies were old enough to vote against him!" she steamed back. A Salt Lake City bookstore removed her books from the window.

She shrugged off insults and abuse hurled from the mouths of people who only wanted to preserve the status quo, who were afraid that any change meant a change for the worse. As she stood before huge crowds where insults poured down as often as applause sounded, she developed a respect for the courageous activists who spoke out no matter what the consequences. Though she sometimes felt bruised and battered by it all, she relished her role in the movement.

"The young ones are coming up with an attitude that says we got it all," she once said. "The older generation still remembers when women didn't think it was respectable to drive alone at night, and went to bed because their husbands were tired."

In May 1980, Erma Bombeck traveled to Salt Lake City to address the National Student Nurses'

Association convention. She arrived in a city that was already stirred up by the Equal Rights Amendment: Sonia Johnson, a feminist Mormon, had been excommunicated by church elders because of her support of the amendment.

Without once looking back, Erma moved in on the controversy, expressing her dissatisfaction with the decision of the Mormon elders. She had sympathy for any woman caught up in a religious battlefield. "I'm gratified that I don't have to choose between God and my conscience." She added that the Mormons' contention that ERA would endanger the family as an institution was "illogical."

"If there were a formula for having a wonderful family," she said, "and that formula said 'get rid of ERA,' I'd probably be first in line. But I don't think you can use the ERA as a dumping ground for all the problems the family is having."

As usual, she shuttled between seriousness and humor. "I would classify myself as a nonviolent mother of three unplanned children. I've been married to the same man for thirty-one years, with whom I've never had a meaningful conversation in my entire life. I iron by demand, have a daughter who is twenty-six years old and has no curiosity as to how to turn on a stove. And I have two sons who make Cain and Abel look like Donny and Marie Osmond."

But then she got down to business and addressed the equal rights controversy. "We've got to get sex out of the gutter and back into the Constitution where it belongs," she said. "The ERA cause— 'equality of rights under the law'—may be the most misunderstood words since 'one size fits all.'"

She repeated her main concern about the women's liberation movement: "I liken the ERA to a war in which they forgot to invite the housewives. I volunteered. No one approached me and said, 'Bombeck, get out and lend your name to this thing.'"

She got excellent publicity for her Utah appearance, both in *People* magazine and in the newspapers. Frank W. Martin at *People* pointed out that Bombeck was not the only person trying to carve out a place for herself among the housewives in the country. "Though they are dissimilar in most respects," he wrote, "[Bombeck] knows that a major competitor in her quest for the support of the silent majority is anti-ERA militant Phyllis Schlafly."

Asked once if she would ever debate Phyllis Schlafly, Erma retorted, "You can't talk to Phyllis on a one-to-one basis. She does a monologue on you. She does a good job of selling herself and has a strong power base. If I left this earth tomorrow, there would be a few million to take my place. If the same thing happened to Phyllis, I can't think of a replacement."

In the long run, it was a bitter disappointment for Erma Bombeck when the Equal Rights Amendment failed in 1982, never to be revived again. She had worked hard on it because she believed in it, but she had been unable to make it succeed.

CHAPTER ELEVEN

∽

Maggie

In spite of the ups and downs, in 1978 Erma Bombeck was hot. Despite the fact that the made-for-TV movie of *The Grass Is Always Greener over the Septic Tank* was a critical disappointment, ABC-TV offered Erma another deal; they wanted her to develop a situation comedy for television. Though she was still busy with her three-times-a-week column and her appearances on *Good Morning America,* she sat down immediately and hammered out the basic idea for a weekly sitcom. The concept was quickly pitched to Marcy Carsey and Tom Werner, the producers who today can claim a number of TV hits, including *The Cosby Show.*

Carsey and Warner liked Erma's idea. Erma had even written a sample script for the show. Although she knew nothing about writing an outline or a working script, she had done both with apparent success.

Basically, Erma wrote herself and her husband into a sitcom. It was set in Dayton, Ohio. Erma made the mother of the family in Dayton as believable a woman as she could, within the confines of the typical sitcom formula. Erma was trying for down-to-earth types who were struggling with real everyday problems—and frequently lost the battles.

Even though the reaction to her work was uniformly positive, there were a few details that needed attention. Erma held long conferences with the producers and kept returning with the additions and alterations they suggested. A half-hour television script might look short when finished, but there is an awful lot of unseen work involved in creating it.

As yet there was no title for the series, although some were already calling it "Maggie," the name of the housewife in the starring role. A year and a half went by before an acceptable pilot was written. At one point, the story had taken on a slightly different accent. The scene had shifted from the suburban kitchen to a beauty parlor, where, every week, the leading lady would come in to have her hair done and talk about life.

"A beauty shop is a very revealing place," Erma was quoted as saying by *The New York Times*. "People are so candid and frank there." She said that she had patterned her sitcom shop on the shop she used to go to in Centerville, Ohio—complete with "pink poodle wallpaper on foil."

The subjects under discussion in the beauty shop would be "men, kids, and their status in life, how abused and put upon they are. It's pretty much the same things men talk about in bars. The only difference is that they don't care about who won the pennant."

But with further consultation, that setting was somewhat modified, and the story line turned back to the original theme: the suburban housewife and her family in the home.

Finally, everything was set. The pilot was cast, and the series would debut in the 1981 fall season. About this time, a sudden change occurred. The executive producer of the series had made another pilot that year, and that pilot was now locked into the fall schedule too, so he would have to leave Erma Bombeck's show. But Hollywood was crawling

with veteran executive producers temporarily between jobs; it would take only minutes to find a
replacement. To Erma's surprise, ABC-TV decided
to offer her the job.

There was no question that she had become a big
name. Ironically, the failure of the made-for-TV
movie *Grass* had made her name a successful staple.
Her only credit in the show had been as creator
and scriptwriter, but who in Hollywood paid any
attention to creators or scriptwriters? It was a coup
for the network to have a big name like Erma
Bombeck as the executive producer of the show.

Erma accepted the job. The only problem was
that she would have to leave Phoenix to work in
Hollywood. It was not exactly what she wanted to
do, but as executive producer she could not run an
operation by telephone a thousand miles away. And
so she and Bill Bombeck talked it over.

Bill had retired from his job as a school admin-
istrator in Phoenix two years before and was now
acting as Erma's business manager. He handled all
the money and frequently went with her on her
lecture trips or other business appointments.

The three children, now twenty-eight, twenty-six,
and twenty-two, had grown up and left home. The
way seemed clear for Bill either to accompany

Erma to the coast or to stay in Phoenix and become a housesitter.

In the end the two of them worked out a simple arrangement. Erma knew she could work during the weekdays in Los Angeles and fly home for the weekends. Thus they would not have to close up the house or rent it out or do anything that might complicate their lives.

Erma Bombeck made the move to Los Angeles not without a smidgeon of reluctance. Pulling up stakes like that and building a whole new life alone in a new city was not the easiest thing for her to do. Besides, Bill was retired. Shouldn't she be retiring too? And yet—she couldn't quit now. Not when she was on a real roll. She knew that a great many people were counting on her. Even if she didn't know quite what she had gotten herself into, she would do the best she could by all the people around her.

Her first few days were a mad whirlwind of activity. She had never been able to acclimate herself to a new place immediately, especially when the move required driving.

On her first trip to Los Angeles, she flew into the Burbank Airport, but she had a difficult time finding the studio from there. The following week she switched to Los Angeles International Airport, thinking that the trip would be easier. Although she followed the directions she was given, she made one wrong turn and found herself at Santa Monica Beach. Carefully retracing her steps, she eventually found her way to Studio City, and drove that route every day. Later she claimed, "I have a way to get from the studio to home, and if that street is ever closed, so help me I'll never get back."

She quickly settled into a mad routine. At five A.M. she got up to dash off one of her columns. She ate breakfast and drove to Studio City, arriving there by nine A.M., where she would work on the scripts for the show and take care of any other details that might come up. As executive producer, she would oversee run-throughs, dress rehearsals, and editing until nine P.M., at which time she would drive back to her apartment and fall into bed. Seemingly minutes later it would be five A.M. again, and she would repeat the whole process.

Then, on Friday nights, she would return her rented car to the airport and fly home to Phoenix and Bill. After that welcome respite, she would be on the move again, flying back to L.A. on Sunday night. She adhered to this backbreaking routine for four months.

The network had ordered thirteen episodes of the show. At the end of the thirteenth show, the network would decide whether to renew or cancel it. Meanwhile, the show, which would be called *Maggie* after all, was shaping up well.

The star was an actress named Miriam Flynn. She would be the TV version of Erma Bombeck, or Maggie Weston, as she was called in the script. The Weston household would include her husband Len, played by actor James Hampton, and three sons: Mark, twelve, played by Billy Jacoby; Bruce, eight, played by Christian Jacobs; and L.J., sixteen, who was never seen because he had moved into the bathroom for good. It was Maggie's belief that these four males were involved in an insidious plot to destroy her sanity and alphabetize her spice rack—which amounted to the same thing.

But Maggie was not a trapped housewife. She escaped the confines of her kitchen by visiting her good friend Loretta, played by Doris Roberts, who ran Loretta's House of Coiffures. At Loretta's, the women talked about toilet training, Brussels sprouts, and other household issues.

In 1981, Erma discussed the show with journalist Holly Miller: "Maggie's not one of those little plastic housewives you can't watch if you're a diabetic.

No one smiles and feeds her kids cookies all the time like on *The Brady Bunch*. The life of a house-wife isn't like that. The problems never resolve themselves, the day never comes out even, and the kids don't turn up wonderful at the end of twenty-four minutes. Maggie's as real as the censors will permit her to be. I've had to fight to keep her real."

Erma explained to her interviewer that TV censors suffered from what she called the "good ol' boy syndrome," meaning that they liked their women dressed in den-mothers' uniforms handing out apple pie, both feet planted firmly on a pedestal.

She told the censors that women were sick of being on that pedestal. " 'Let them be real,' I said. 'Let Maggie be tired once in a while; let her say she's sick of always getting the bent fork and eating the egg with the broken yolk.' The whole concept was questionable to them."

She won the fight, she explained to Holly Miller, and Maggie had all the quirks and tics of a thir-tyish homemaker from Ohio. She was married to a high school vice principal; she was the mother of three boys. It was life with the Bombecks, but the similarity ended right there.

"Maggie's living in the 1980s, and her attitudes

are a lot different than mine were when I was thirty. Sure, there's some of me in Maggie, but she stands alone. She has anger; she has hostility; she vacillates between loving her children and wanting to sell them; she worries about age and the fact that she has a cookie sheet older than her gynecologist."

Erma even came clean with Holly Miller about the reason she chose to take on such an added burden when she was doing so well with her print contracts. "It's the challenge."

"What else is in it for me, really? I don't need the aggravation, and I certainly don't need the money to live on. I've lived on a lot less and have been just as happy. I like to work; that's where I get my fulfillment. Woody Allen had a line I gobbled up once. He said if you're not failing, you're not trying anything. I read that and thought he was talking to me. He didn't mean we should go out and court failure but that we need to take risks once in a while."

It was the challenge, but there was more to it than that. Erma finally confessed that she had really given up something of herself in all those years of working. "I've given up the ability to fill in my time with something that's really relaxing. I don't play very well; that's what I'm trying to say, I get very restless. I'm not a beach person. I know people who just lie there and watch the ocean come in. I want to fix it if it has a leak. I want to build something on the shore."

She now felt that she had built something good. She told the interviewer, "Sometimes if they're looking at the history of our times and wondering about the vast group of people who lived and raised kids in the suburbs, this is as close a chronicle as they're going to get." She was talking about *Maggie*. "This is the way we felt, the way we lived, and the way things really were. It's pretty close to the truth."

Maggie debuted in September 1981 and survived for eight weeks. There was no specific reason for its cancellation; the show just did not get the ratings it needed to survive. Many shows each season are canceled before they are deeply rooted—or get a chance to be. That was the fate of *Maggie*.

As for Erma, she decided that she had never really acclimated herself to showbiz talk—"That one doesn't work for me, sweetie, trust me!"—and wouldn't be missing much to leave Hollywood behind.

What surprised Erma more than anything was

the cavalier way the people in the show accepted the cancellation. While she was not hurt by the show's failure, she was sorry for the people around her who were now jobless. It intrigued her to see that most actors and technicians were usually not too shocked at anything that might happen in the course of their careers.

The press bothered her the most. Interviewers asked her what she thought about being a failure. Erma was not a thin-skinned creative person who let the critics ruin her confidence. When she started on *Maggie,* she knew that the chances of success were very thin. After all, she saw what had happened to *Grass* with Carol Burnett. Now *there* was a pro who had been caught in something that didn't really work out well. Was she any different?

It is interesting to note that 1981, the year *Maggie* debuted, was called "the worst season in boob-tube history." In fact, almost none of the shows launched that season made it through the year to be re-scheduled for the following season.

In Erma's case, she had made lots of friends, and had had a unique experience. There was a great deal of camaraderie in the business of television and filmmaking. As a writer, the most solitary profession of them all, Erma had never enjoyed much sociability. When she filmed her spots for ABC-TV, she dealt strictly with technicians, and, while they were friendly, they were not like actors and writers.

She had found a great deal of friendship in the few months she had spent on *Maggie*. The excitement of working up a script, the joy of seeing her own words come to life, the rush of watching a scene come off after she had worked on it for so long: these were not things she could experience alone at the typewriter. She was glad for the chance to have had these experiences.

Finally it was cleanup time. Erma had brought in some of her own furniture to use on the show, which now had to be packed up and shipped back to Phoenix.

She was on the set trying to figure out how to begin this massive and exhausting cleanup when someone appeared in the semidarkness. It was Bill, Erma's husband. He had taken the first plane from Phoenix when she had called the night before. He wanted to help her clean things up. They got the furniture tagged for loading and then went to Erma's small apartment, where he helped her clean the kitchen floor. As they locked up and prepared to leave, Bill looked at her wonderingly, and said, "I just don't know how you do it. You move to a big city, you meet new people, you do a job you never did before. Alone. That's the sign of a successful woman. Tell you what, before we fly home, let's take a drive out to the ocean at Santa Monica. Which way do I go?"

Erma laughed. "The only way I can get there is from the airport. That's where I make my wrong turn."

CHAPTER TWELVE

Paradise Valley

In the fall of 1980, when Erma was struggling valiantly to get *Maggie* off the ground, and *Aunt Erma's Cope Book* was well on its way to becoming a best-seller, Erma Bombeck couldn't have been busier.

In addition to pulling together a script for *Maggie* and publicizing *Aunt Erma's Cope Book*, Erma had yet another project ready in the wings. Actually, it was not a project that she was involved in doing herself. But it did touch her tangentially.

A television writer named Susan Silver approached Erma with an original idea: she wanted to use *Aunt Erma's Cope Book* as the background for a play about Erma Bombeck titled "Erma." Susan Silver had a good track record in television. She was one of the original writers for *The Mary Tyler Moore Show,* and she had written scripts for the sitcom *Maude.* One of her first suggestions for the part of Erma Bombeck was Bea Arthur, who had played *Maude,* Edith Bunker's cousin, in Norman Lear's sitcom *All in the Family.*

Two Broadway producers, Larry Kasha and David Landay, were commissioned to produce the show. "The play is a satire on modern life," Kasha told *New York Times* writer Carol Lawson. "The structure of the play is very free form—a series of vignettes." He explained, "Erma talks to the audience, as George Burns did in the old Burns and Allen TV shows. Susan Silver has created a story line to link the vignettes together. There are sequences about people jogging, going through therapy—whatever the latest fad is."

To clarify the concept a little more, Kasha explained, "There is one scene showing how you can't have a simple dinner party anymore. You can't seat environmentalists with conservationists, smokers with nonsmokers."

Susan Silver lived in Los Angeles at the time, but

she was making frequent trips to Erma's home in Phoenix to confer with her on the script. "Erma has been wonderfully helpful," Kasha told Carol Lawson. "She has final approval of the script."

The meetings between Erma and Susan continued for months, and the script gradually took shape. Because she was also struggling to make a television script take shape for her sitcom *Maggie*, Erma could see how hard it was to make any script come to life, be it for stage or for the small screen.

"We wanted a woman to write this play," Kasha noted. "We felt that a woman would have more rapport with Bombeck's material. Besides, Susan is going through the same midlife crisis herself."

We'll never know whether or not it would have been a success, for the project was abandoned in the fall of 1980. Erma had the same reaction to the failure of "Erma" as she had later on to the failure of *Maggie*. It was not that she was a failure, but that she had made a mistake. In the case of "Erma" the play, she wasn't personally responsible. There were dozens of people involved in the Broadway project. She was simply the featured star of the show even though she was not acting in it. Though the sudden disappearance of the show gave Erma pause, she recovered quickly, always ready to come back with a smile and a laugh. But it was time to think about something else.

By now, of course, the kids had long ago left the "nest." For some time, Erma and Bill had been wanting to change their surroundings just a little. When they had moved to Phoenix they had bought a house that was already built. What they wanted now was a home custom-made for them. And eventually a wonderful home emerged, one that Erma simply loved. She had never loved her other homes. She had tolerated them. She had lived in them. She had worked in them. She had made her fortune in them. But she had never *loved* any of them like this. "I never want to leave this house," she said, after moving in.

The Bombeck's house had a distinctly Spanish influence. It was situated on a large piece of land overlooking Paradise Valley. The house and grounds were extensive. They included a tennis court, a garden where Erma could work, and a waterfall. The interior of the house was full of pleasant surprises. It was colorful without being garish, and cluttered without being terribly hard to get around in.

There were terra-cotta floors with a Southwestern-

Spanish motif. The furniture was hand-painted and sometimes built to order. The Bombecks also fancied stone sculptures of all kinds, which were strewn throughout the house. The rugs covering the terra-cotta floors were mostly Persians, thick and colorful. There were even lamps made out of seashells. But Erma's prize was her bed, which featured a Mexican tin headboard.

The house was a marvel, but sometimes the extra space only served to remind her of her children's absence. She had developed a kind of philosophy about them—a philosophy she explained to Cindy Adams. "I can remember when my kids were little and they'd come home from school wanting something and I'd simply have to say, 'Hey, later. I'm writing now.' Okay, so it's fifty pounds of guilt on me, but I can take that. The writing comes first.

"The fact is, I've always wanted to write. When I was a kid in school I wanted to write. It's all I ever wanted to do. I never wanted to do any of those greatly heroic things like nursing. I wanted to shut myself off and write real, real early. As a result, my kids often had to fend for themselves.

"But they still had a good life even though I sometimes left them on their own. They each had a shot at college. They didn't end up stealing hubcaps. They never served time. They aren't weird. They turned out decent, so obviously, I wasn't a bad mother."

Erma would always remember the night she appeared on the *Tonight Show*. During the commercial break, Johnny Carson leaned over to her and said in a low tone, "Any of your kids in the slammer?" Erma assured him that they were not. Carson said, "It's a good week then, isn't it?"

Erma agreed: "I measure a good week by if their cars are running and they're not in the slammer. Really, though, they are three individual kids who have found happiness doing what they are happy doing." She elaborated: "They're healthy and happy, and we're still a close family. And that's the best you can hope for."

When she was not writing, Erma puttered around the house and occasionally worked in the garden. "I love to garden and dig in the dirt. I cook and listen to Dan Rather at the same time. We have a housekeeper four days a week, but still, my husband does the dishes. Then I watch anything that moves on television while I needlepoint. About ten o'clock I get in bed, read for a while and that's it.

"As for the kids, when they come home, I put them up in the guest room. And that's the key word, *guest* room. Eventually I deliver my 'You know we love you, but...' speech. It's not that I want to, but I really have to tell them to pick themselves up and get out. I mean, it's great staying home with Mama. The laundry is done, the refrigerator is stocked, the telephone bills are ours.

"It is my feeling that the children should not live with us at their age." At the time of this remark, her daughter Betsy was thirty-two, her son Andy was thirty, and her son Matt, twenty-eight. "They just have to learn to make their own way. They'll never have the opportunity to find out how good they are if they cling to us, if they don't do it themselves. I only mean to help them, and right or wrong, that's my philosophy.

"Maybe it's a little bit selfish, but at this stage of our lives, it's really better for my husband and me to be by ourselves. We're entitled to listen to our own music and to use our own car when we want to and to know that when the phone rings, it's for us."

Erma Bombeck always helped out local causes as well as national ones. In Phoenix in February 1981, she participated in a formal black-tie dinner-dance at seventy-five dollars a head to raise money for the March of Dimes's fight against birth defects.

Erma was also one of eleven local celebrities to

take part in a cook-off that was judged by a panel including *New York Times* gourmet editor Craig Claiborne. Other celebrities involved were Amanda Black, *Gunsmoke*'s Miss Kitty, and Jane Wyatt, the film actress.

Erma Bombeck was one of the cooks. "That rumor that I can't cook is just a big, ugly myth," she told Dorothee Polson of the *Arizona Republic*. "I've heard those stories, that all I can make is rock soup; that punishment for my children was being sent to bed with dinner." She shook her head adamantly, pursing her lips. "Not true. Cooking is my life. I even take gourmet cooking classes." Bombeck jokingly explained exactly how she defined gourmet dishes. "That's recipes written with words that you can't understand, calling for ingredients that you can't get."

Erma explained to the newspaper reporter covering the event how she had finally gotten into the world of cooking. While she had never had the slightest curiosity over what occurred in the kitchen when she was young, once she was married and suddenly had mouths to feed, she realized she might need to learn. She invented a system of feeding, which she called the "trough" system. "I cooked a lot of macaroni and cheese or anything that would fatten them up."

About the upcoming cook-off, she said, "Even though gala guests will be allowed to talk with us while we're cooking, I don't anticipate being nervous. Even if I cut myself, I'll keep signing autographs, probably with my own blood."

When the reporter asked Erma what her husband thought about her cooking, she retorted spiritedly, "What does he know?"

Erma Bombeck's seventh book, *Motherhood: The Second Oldest Profession,* came out in late 1983. Although she had been churning out best-sellers for some years, Erma still had stage fright when she visited a bookstore to sign copies, since she was never sure anyone would show up.

She recalled that once, in a Marshall Field Department Store in Chicago, "I could not bring myself to look up and see if there was anyone in line. I looked at my feet and hoped to God somebody would be there who didn't work for the store." Her fears were unfounded; nearly fifteen hundred people lined up for her signature.

Her *Motherhood* book tour took her all over the country. In one store she recorded a message that was played over the loudspeaker system: "Come see Erma Bombeck and she'll sign her new book for you. Or, on the other hand, stay home. Your son might call."

Her personal appearances were great for book sales. After a few months, *Motherhood* was anchored at the top of the best-seller lists, with 800,000 copies in print.

Erma joked about the huge number of people who waited in line for her signature: "One woman came up to me and I said, 'Oh, your baby is adorable.' She said, 'Thank you. It was born in the line.'"

The book was a smash hit, selling nearly one million copies in hardcover.

A satire of motherhood, the book included a meeting of television's supermoms of a past era such as Donna from *The Donna Reed Show* and Harriet from *Ozzie and Harriet* in which the role models finally turned human. Another chapter showed what happened when a man traded places with his wife to become a male mother. There was also a chapter titled "Everybody Else's Mother"— the mom that kids claimed *always* let her kids do what they wanted.

Even Erma's author biography was funny: "Erma

Bombeck writes a humor column three times a week for 900 newspapers from her home in Paradise Valley, Arizona. She appears twice a week on ABC's *Good Morning America*. She has a loving husband and three children who have never published a book about her. She calls her Mom and Dad at least once a week and holds ten honorary degrees. Her husband comes home every day and asks, 'So what have you been doing all day?'"

CHAPTER THIRTEEN

∾

"Anyone Home?"

In 1985 the Tournament of Roses Association—the organization that runs the Rose Bowl Parade just prior to the Rose Bowl Football Game in Pasadena, California—selected their motto for the coming New Year's parade. it was "A Celebration of Laughter."

As soon as the motto was chosen, the association began looking for a grand marshal, an honor given each year to the person who best exemplified that year's theme. No journalist had ever been chosen to lead the prestigious parade, the granddaddy of all New Year's parades. But in 1985, the Tournament of Roses Association honored Erma Bombeck.

Erma naturally accepted the offer, which she felt was just another challenge for a shy person who preferred to hide behind her typewriter. As grand marshal, she joined the ranks of a number of celebrities, three former presidents of the United States, and many other luminaries from the worlds of show business and politics.

A journalist jokingly asked Erma if she thought the standards for the Rose Bowl Parade were going up or down. "Are you crazy?" Erma shot back. "This is breaking ground here. They may not be able to equal this ever again."

She admitted that she was "shocked, amazed, awed, and excited" by the prospects—in exactly that order. She also said that the parade's theme was absolutely perfect, a motto she had devoted her life to. "I think laughter is just about the most important thing in the world. And besides, parades, along with dust collecting, have always been a favorite hobby of mine." She added, "Actually, what I *really* wanted was to be named Queen of the Rose Bowl"—an honor that usually went to the winner of a beauty contest. She shook her head. "I just couldn't hold my breath to hold in my stomach for two hours."

It was the ninety-seventh Rose Bowl Parade.

Erma served as grand marshal of the ceremony, riding with her husband Bill and her three grown children, who saluted the huge crowds that packed the streets of Pasadena along Foothill Boulevard.

In 1986 Erma Bombeck had an unpleasant announcement for ABC-TV. She had decided that her weekly appearances on *Good Morning America,* which had debuted on November 3, 1975, were getting to be just a little too much for her to handle. Therefore, she announced that she would be quitting the spot on Thursday morning, September 25. She said she had absolutely no complaints with ABC-TV, but that her increasing workload was simply making it impossible for her to appear twice a week. "It's the best job I've ever had, but I'm walking away from it," she admitted.

She also said that she was preparing a play for Broadway and writing a new book. In turn, ABC-TV said that they were extremely sorry to be losing her, and that she would be welcome on the program whenever she was in New York.

The Broadway play she said she was working on was never produced. She had originally visualized her book *Motherhood* as a play, but this vision was never realized.

Dropping her television work did not signal a

change in Erma Bombeck's writing style or in her attitude about her work. But some things had changed a great deal. Though the lifestyle that Erma Bombeck had satirized and parodied during the sixties and seventies was not gone, it had changed significantly. But there was also a wrenching change in Erma's own family: The kids had all left home.

There were things that were still funny about the kitchen, and the kids, even though they were absent. But Erma may have begun to wonder if her material was starting to seem dated. Was she losing something by sticking with the same territory?

In September 1987, Erma Bombeck was asked to introduce Pope John Paul II, who would be presiding over a papal Mass in Sun Devil Stadium, Tempe, Arizona. "I was humbled by the honor," Erma wrote, "and wanted desperately to do something special. I decided to welcome him in Polish, his native tongue."

Erma remembered that the priest who had married her and Bill was Polish, too, and thought this might be a good sign. She called up a seamstress she knew who spoke Polish. "Tell me how to welcome the pope in his own language," she asked her friend.

The woman obliged her. Studying the unfamiliar words was difficult, but Erma memorized the greeting and was ready for the pope's arrival. That night, she rehearsed the speech before a couple of priests in charge of the event. Erma's speech went something like this? *"Arizona vita oitsa sven-tego yana pavwa druuuuuuuugeggo."*

One of the priests turned to Erma, slightly puzzled. "Why would you want to tell the pope his luggage is lost?" he asked with a twinkle in his eye. In the end, the diction was straightened out, and Erma was able to greet the pope with the proper words in her somewhat halting Polish.

For her eighth book, Erma gathered together some of her columns during the year or so between books and looked them over. She saw in a flash what the book's theme should be—family visits. And so the book *Family: The Ties That Bind...And Gag!* began to take on some shape. It was published in 1987. *Publishers Weekly* liked it. "Syndicated columnist and best-selling author [Erma] Bombeck here takes a look at the family grown and comes up with characteristically incisive, irreverent and pertinent wisdom.

"Adult children who return to the empty nest, technology that needs to be mastered in kitchen and family room are grist for Bombeck's ever-ready mill. 'Family is a perennial that comes up year after year' demonstrates matriarch Bombeck."

The book's dedication to Bill Bombeck amused one reviewer, Joyce Slater of the *Chicago Tribune.* "To Bill Bombeck, who had definite ideas of the conception of these characters long before I had ideas of putting them into a book." The "characters" in question were the Bombeck children. The quip was typical Bombeck—just a trifle naughty, but nothing overbearing or tasteless.

Slater went on to describe the book as a more or less "good-natured grumble." "Some problems are timeless; others are products of the more sophisticated, microchip eighties. All demonstrate [Erma's] deft touch and her ability to find humor in the peskiest situations."

She cited Erma's frustration with family vacations: "I was not likely to forget the hitchhiker who, after twenty miles, wrote us a check to let him out...how I envied him."

In response to Bill Bombeck's futile campaign to economize, Erma wrote, "For thirty years he had dedicated his life to flipping off lights in rooms with no one in them, turning off water spigots in the bathroom and throwing his body over the meter in an effort to stop the dials from spinning." No wonder, Erma quipped, that he was known to his friends as the "Prince of Darkness." She also joked about her family's love of VCRs: "Already we're beginning to cut corners. We've got *60 Minutes* down to thirty, *20/20* down to ten/ten, and anything on World War II we fast-forward because we know the ending."

Time magazine called *Family* "an amiable reworking of her familiar material," and went on to say that if "she were accurately reporting the changes in her own life, she would admit that she no longer has to count the crumbs in cracker-box suburbia. If state-fair-quality dust balls grow anywhere in her snazzy Arizona rancho, it is in the box with those twelve honorary doctorates."

But in the end, *Time* admitted, "Bombeck knows what she is doing, and she honors the passage of time by retelling beloved old knee-slappers. Her son, now grown, comes home for a visit, throws the door open, and just the way he used to fifteen years ago, looks her in the eye and asks, 'Anyone home?' Her adult kids still lock themselves in the bathroom till the dishes are done. Leftovers? Sure, but we roar for more."

The *Time* review was fair in its criticisms; Bombeck

was rehashing old material—but it was *funny* old material, and people didn't want her to change.

People's Joanne Kaufman was less enthusiastic: "Bombeck traverses the same territory she has covered in previous books...in syndicated columns, and in her appearances on *Good Morning America....* Bombeck has never come close to Jean Kerr as a chronicler of domestic dementia, and with *Family* the gap widens."

Magill Book Reviews reported, "[The family's] experiences, and Bombeck's reflections upon them, are sometimes hilarious, sometimes moving, but always entertaining." Though warning that her humor could be "wearying in large doses," the reviewer wrote, "An essential purchase for all Erma Bombeck fans, this book will provide hours of enjoyment to parents and children young and old."

Erma's life was no longer simple, and sometimes it required deep discipline. "I'm very disciplined. My secretary, Norma, who is in four hours a week, handles phones. I'm at the typewriter with the door closed until noon, and I don't stop working for anybody. Then I break for a quick lunch, which I make myself. It's something light, like an open-face sandwich or a cup of soup. After that it's a half-hour nap, then I'm back hitting it again until five-thirty."

For all the hoopla associated with being a celebrity writer, the writing was still the most important thing in her life. She was amused by wannabe writers. "I get people who tell me they want to write, too, but that they have this house, and they have these kids, and they have that car pool. Listen, the priority has to be this, right at the top. People can't put their dreams in a little box and take them out and play with them from time to time. These are people who are afraid to put it on the line."

An established success, a millionaire even, she knew exactly who and where she was. But she knew the critics were right about *Family*. It was a lot of the same old stuff all over again. She tried to keep it fresh—but was that possible, given the way she thought and turned out her material?

She had quit her job with ABC-TV in order to give herself a little more quality time—but it turned out that she just spent more time writing. There was nothing wrong with that, except that maybe she was getting into a rut.

Although she had been a celebrity for a long time, she still had a sense of insecurity left over from her youth. "Celebrity status is hard for me," she confessed. "And looking good is something I can't do either. I know that when I walk into a room, I don't stand out. I disappoint people when they see me in person. I just know it.

"I'm always shorter than they expected. They're so disappointed by my size, they always tell me, 'Oh, I thought you were taller!' So I say, 'Well, I write tall.' I don't know what else to say to them. Of course, I shouldn't feel such pressure. I should be secure enough not to have to prove anything, but it's a matter of trying to please everyone."

Even with all the money and the adulation, Erma felt that she had never been able to develop dramatic *presence*—the thing actors and actresses have that makes them different from most people. "Some people have great style," she remarked once. "I'm thinking of James Garner, who always seems to say the right thing and keep it all in proper perspective. But I've gone to give speeches and people don't know who I am. Like when I was booked once for Lancaster, Ohio, I walked in, and they asked for my ticket. I said, 'I'm the speaker,' and you could see them thinking, Dear Lord, we've got to suffer through *this* for the next hour?"

Once, she was standing outside a New York City hotel, waiting for a taxi. A photographer beside her suddenly asked her to move just a little to the left, indicating where he wanted her to stand. Erma obliged, all fidgety and excited. He was going to take her picture! Maybe she'd be in the New York paper the next day!

"Oh, yes, yes," said Erma, striking a pose. The photographer aimed his camera just behind Erma, at a man with a dog on a leash. Erma turned to the doorman. "Who's that man?" she asked. The doorman answered her as if she were daft. "Not the man. The dog! *Time* magazine is taking a picture of the dog—Mike—from *Down and Out in Beverly Hills.*" She thought, "Well, it's sure all over for you, honey. That's it. Finished. Your career's right down the toilet."

Erma was dejected by this episode, but these things seemed to happen to her frequently. "I can walk into a room with my mother, and it's my mother who will get all the attention," Erma said. "People will walk up to her and say, 'I thought your daughter was coming with you,' and she'll say, 'My daughter *is* with me. She's the one sitting by the chip dip.' I don't stand out. And, certainly not when my mother's around.

"My mom is incredible. She can walk into a strange bookstore and tell them who she is and rearrange their displays to put my book in front. She'll regale the people with stories. She has this great sense of freedom that I admire, even though I don't have it."

Despite her success, Erma felt that something was missing in her life. For years, she and Bill had spent a lot of their spare time traveling around the world. It was therapy for Erma, and Bill loved to travel, too. So the Bombecks began a long succession of travels around the globe. It was all part of Erma's self-searching.

In the end, Erma laughed when she realized she had gone on a global search for herself, to find out where she should go next, but found the answers to her questions right in Arizona, not too far from home.

CHAPTER FOURTEEN

❧

The Camp with a Difference

Camp Sunrise, located a few miles from the town of Payson, Arizona, was a camp with a difference: The kids at Camp Sunrise all had cancer. Because cancer experts had decided that grouping kids with cancer together in a fun environment might help them endure the torments of their disease, a number of camps were constructed in the late 1970s in order to judge their effectiveness.

The experts found that living with other kids with similar problems did make a difference. In addition, the survival rates for patients with cancer had jumped dramatically since the 1960s. The rate of survival for people with lymphocytic leukemia had risen from zero to 60 percent, and for those with Hodgkin's disease, from 50 to 90 percent.

Camp Sunrise taught the kids that there was a way to beat cancer. This change of philosophy swept through the camps, and the survival rates were astonishingly high everywhere.

A woman named Ann Wheat was the director of Camp Sunrise. She was also assistant director of Arizona Childhood Cancer Services. She was dissatisfied with the books that had been written about kids with cancer. The reason was obvious. At the time most of the books had been written, the cancer survival rate for children was at its lowest. The books were all dedicated to showing children how to die—or, at best, how to make the most of their last few hours. The philosophy was wrong. She wanted books to show them how to live as normally as they could, to face their problems with others just like them.

Ann Wheat knew that these kids were no different from kids at any normal summer camp. Despite medication and special treatments, a kid is still a kid—and, in spite of disease, most kids act normal.

Ann Wheat wanted a new book that would show kids how to live with their illness as best they could and enjoy their lives as much as possible.

She was familiar with Erma Bombeck's writing, and thought that what was really missing from the outdated books was humor—the thing Erma was famous for. Of course she understood that it was not easy to make cancer funny, but she wrote a letter to Erma Bombeck, inviting her to have lunch with her to discuss a project, which she did not describe. Erma agreed, completely in the dark. She never refused to do something that might help out someone else.

Ann Wheat described the situation at Camp Sunrise, suggesting that Erma might be able to help her improve the morale of the kids during their first days at Camp Sunrise, as they became acclimated to the place. Could Erma write a small pamphlet that would give the new kids an insight into the camp's activities?

Erma thought she might help out somehow, but she wondered why Ann Wheat had selected her for the job. Weren't there experts in cancer? The trouble with the experts, Ann Wheat said, was that they thought in terms of cancer. They did not think in kids' terms. Erma knew kids; she had studied them all her life. The scientists also lacked *humor*.

That was why Ann Wheat had really selected Erma.

At first, Erma was appalled. It was definitely against her principles to laugh at people who were crippled or suffered from any infirmity. It was simply not *nice* to make fun of disease and death. No, she said, it would be impossible.

At the end of the meal, Ann Wheat invited Erma to drive out to Camp Sunrise the following week for a visit. It wouldn't mean agreeing to write the pamphlet, it would simply be a gift from Ann Wheat and the kids at Camp Sunrise.

In a way, Erma was shamed into making a trip down to Payson, Arizona. She went reluctantly, afraid of what she might see in the eyes of those kids. She was surprised to find some of the kids looking as healthy as any she might see in her own neighborhood. There were others, of course, who were crippled. Some were pale and bald. Others limped noticeably. As she talked to them, she realized that no one had given in to self-pity. In fact, they were all simply there to fight their disease with every treatment available to them. They wanted to *live*.

Erma's pity for the children had all but dissolved.

They didn't need it. Half the battle for a cancer victim was finding the self-assurance to beat the disease. These kids had that self-assurance. They knew they were going to weather their illness. The sound of kids laughing astounded her. There was as much laughter here as there was on an ordinary school playground, she realized. And these were kids afflicted with incurable diseases! How did they do it?

There was a courage here that even cancer could not defeat. They knew the odds against them. They knew the pain, discouragement, and loss of dignity they faced. They knew what they were missing, and yet they laughed.

Ann Wheat wanted a pamphlet featuring something "to give them a shot of optimism." This kind of humor was not up Erma's alley at all—it was the black humor of the alienated, and her sunny, humorous bent did not exactly fit that category.

She decided to talk to the kids, pull some statistics together, and knock out a pamphlet that would give them a shot of Bombeck-flavored optimism. And she did just that. She talked to the kids, often brainstorming with groups of them, and she came up with a number of funny things involving their treatments. The kids said that they wanted the first chapter to be called "Am I Gonna Die?" because that was what everyone wanted to know when they were first diagnosed.

Erma was astonished that the kids refused to be horrified by their illnesses. They ignored their symptoms whenever possible, hoping for a bright tomorrow and laughing today. It taught Erma a memorable lesson. "If you can't handle optimism, don't hang around children with cancer."

She was already having trouble trying to shape up her pamphlet when the news that she was writing a funny book about cancer leaked out. She got thousands of letters from people who had cancer victims in their families. Most of the letters were painful and sad, and did not really exhibit the dark humor she was trying to get from her camp kids.

Nevertheless, she finally managed to write three chapters, although she was unhappy with the material. She was trying to blend humor with grim realism—and somehow it didn't seem to work.

She took it to Camp Sunrise and read it aloud to the kids. When she finished there was silence. Erma waited for the kids to praise the way she had captured their experiences, the way that she had portrayed them as courageous and self-assured.

179

Instead the kids shook their heads. "It's okay, but it's got to be funnier. This is not funny." Automatically, Erma scrawled the word "funnier" on her yellow legal pad as she looked at them carefully.

Funny, she thought. She was the expert on funny, and yet she had apparently missed the boat here. As she read over what she had written, she realized that she had written herself into the story too much. She was supplying the humor—not the kids. The kids wanted to supply the laughs themselves.

She began her interviews with the kids all over again. This time, she dove under the surface to find out what the kids themselves thought about their situations. And she began to find nuggets of humor hidden in the background.

"They need the humor," she said. "They need it to survive. It's a little black at times, but it's essential."

When Erma probed the kids about their chemotherapy treatments, she discovered that they had made up a game about it. A very sick game, without question. The teenagers had devised a special contest to see who could wait the longest before throwing up after chemotherapy.

The kids had also made up what they called "Murphy's Medical Law." This "law" read: "The more boring and out-of-date the magazines are in the waiting room, the longer you have to wait for your scheduled appointment." Erma pointed out that a positive attitude toward chemotherapy would not make the treatment unnecessary, but it would improve the quality of day-to-day life during the treatment.

She found most of the humor during the interviews. "When three-year-old Carrie's blond curls were all gone and a little fuzz was starting to grow back, she observed with curiosity her father's balding head as he bent over to tie her shoe. 'Daddy,' she asked, 'is your hair coming or going?'"

As she was composing the pamphlet, Erma knew that she had a good solid book in her—the pamphlet would simply be expanded, but it would include this black humor and the anecdotes the kids had come up with.

The finished book was called *I Want to Grow Hair. I Want to Grow Up. I Want to Go to Boise.* When asked to explain the title, Erma told *Ladies' Home Journal,* "I asked the kids what they'd want if they had three wishes, and I got a lot of the usual: go to Disneyland, own a Porsche." However, one of the kids said, "I want to grow hair. I want to grow up. I want to go to Boise." Erma thought that summed up life pretty well for that one kid. "Hair is a priority because it's so debilitating to them to lose it. And growing up doesn't seem to be too unreasonable to ask. Boise? I don't know. It just amused me so. It was a title that makes you smile and you don't know why."

Working on the book changed Erma more than she had suspected it would. After all, none of her previous books had had such an effect on her. As she described it, "Things that were important before don't seem worth worrying about now. I'm more of a one-day-at-a-time person. I think about the three-year-old boy who threw his arms around me and said, 'You know what? I'm going to the circus!' The counselor corrected him, saying they were going swimming. Without missing a beat, the kid said, 'You know what? I'm going swimming!' It didn't matter, he would have gone to the opening of a bottle of aspirin. And it made me think—little things, little moments. Go for them."

As she finished the book, Erma realized that the thing that kids with cancer needed most was understanding. "They want so badly to be treated as normal. They don't want to stand out. I remember one girl who said she went to school and the teacher looked over to her and said, 'Monica, shut up and sit down.' She told me, 'I just knew it was going to be such a good year.' Someone wasn't going to treat her like an invalid! And they want their disease to be understood.... We have people who still think cancer can be contagious. It's an ignorance that's not addressed. It's just like AIDS."

Erma knew she was changing as she was writing the book. It was a little unnerving. But interviewing these kids gave her a deeper insight into life. She realized for the first time how a cancer victim is not alone in a family. Brothers and sisters suffered as well. In a family with a cancer victim, the rest of the family seems to count very little: all attention is focused on the sick child. Erma knew that her sense of values was shifting.

Working on the book had no effect on her daily columns, however. In fact, she found that being funny every day did not get harder. If anything, it got easier. Still, she did realize that "some days are harder than others. After twenty-five years you do work the same ground, but you come at it from different directions. One thing in my favor is that I'm really insecure; I'm always looking over my shoulder, and I always think it can all go away tomorrow. That works for me because if I ever become complacent and think, Hey, I've got it made, what are they going to do, fire me? The answer is, yes. My contract with each of my seven hundred newspapers is a thirty-day contract. If they don't like what they see, they've got an out. So I live hand-to-mouth."

While writing *I Want to Grow Hair,* Erma realized that while she was still a humor writer, she was also a social commentator. "I take that from the scope of stuff that I do," she explained. "Sometimes I turn serious in a column—I wrote about mothers and retarded children; I do some bittersweet things on which child you love the best. It's not 100 percent humor, because life isn't that way. I like the idea of the readers feeling there's a woman out there who has several sets of feelings. Some days I look at life and say, 'Is this a hoot?' And other days I say, 'This is tough.' I think you give yourself a little more credibility when you do that."

When the book finally appeared in 1989, it was greeted with a variety of reactions. *The New York Times Book Review* hated it. "It's hard to imagine a more well-intentioned book," Ann Banks wrote. "Erma Bombeck has put her considerable talent as a humorist in the service of changing people's attitudes toward children with cancer.... Though her motives are laudable, the uncomfortable truth is that Mrs. Bombeck is in over her head. Having interviewed many children who are surviving cancer, she struggles valiantly to convey their plucky insights. But she isn't able to build a narrative or even tell a sustained anecdote, and her customary shtick is simply not equal to the task."

She concluded, "One sympathizes with Erma Bombeck for having set herself an essentially impossible task. In the war on cancer, she's strictly a civilian. Yes, laughter is valuable medicine, but I suspect that puns about hair loss and quips about chemotherapy work best in the waiting room."

But others applauded her. Doris Reidy in the *Chicago Tribune* concluded her positive review with this observation: "Popular writers are not generally known for their willingness to innovate. So it's a fine thing to see Bombeck march off to a different drummer. It's even finer when it works."

Julie Szekely in *U.S.A. Weekend* wrote, "It is an inspirational book with a single overwhelming message: Kids with cancer may have an adult disease, but they still deserve their childhood."

Publishers Weekly was enthusiastic: "Author of eight best-sellers (*Motherhood: The Second Oldest Profession* et al), TV personality and syndicated columnist, Bombeck soars over her earlier accomplishments with this book…. The 'different-family' stories she relates about extraordinarily brave boys and girls are wildly funny, also ineffably moving…. One admires Bombeck not only for the sensitivity and valor with which she accomplishes this project, but also for her selflessness in donating to cancer research the total of what will surely be considerable royalties earned worldwide from this book."

In 1990, Erma discussed the book at a luncheon given by Ann Wheat. "The important thing to remember is that I couldn't have written this book seven years ago because there were no survivors. Now 60 to 90 percent of these kids survive. There are more winners than losers, and death does not write the final chapter."

All royalties from the book went to the research division of The American Cancer Society. By the time Erma spoke at that luncheon, over a million dollars in royalties had already been given to the society.

CHAPTER FIFTEEN

~

That Perfect Vacation

With Bill Bombeck's retirement, the Bombecks had found their lifestyle increasingly flexible. They had always loved to travel, but now, unencumbered by the presence of their children, they began traveling even more.

An interviewer once asked Erma, "Do you and your husband sit down and actually plan vacations? How does that work?" "It's a lot like the trials at Nuremberg, I suppose," she answered after a bit of thought. "We sit around a little table and we have this conversation and he wants to go on some exotic thing and I want to talk gift shops here. This is pretty much the way we work."

Their ideas about vacations were not too similar. Erma observed, "We have such expectations out of vacations. We really do. We think it's going to do everything. It's going to clear up our skins, it's going to make us wonderful, we're going to lose the stress, we're going to do all that stuff.

"And it doesn't do any of those things. I mean it's pretty much like a death march in most instances. I call it the Peace Corps—with diarrhea."

And yet they continued to travel whenever they could. "We always live in hope that we're going to go on a trip and our luggage is going to get there the same time that we get there and the beach will be great and [my] husband won't argue with [me] and [I] won't get sick and throw up in some sink that's shaped like a seashell—for which [we're] paying $300 a day. And we just live in hope for that perfect vacation—and I'm still looking for it."

But they often found great places—places like Papua, New Guinea, Erma's favorite foreign spot. Why? "Because it was great shopping to begin with.... We go down the Sepik River and I'm looking around, and I don't even smell a gift shop. I'm very worried. I'm having withdrawal. So we hit the shore and then I see all these tamberon houses, and they've got all of these things that they've

sculpted and these wood carvings and these wonderful necklaces and things and I think: So—it's all
for sale! So I go up to this little man and I say,
'How much?' In any language it works. How much?
And he says, 'First price, three hundred dollars.
Second price, thirty dollars.' And then he waits. I
said, 'What's he waiting for?' I mean—give me the
second price! This was like paradise."

The Bombecks weren't fans of cruise ships,
though. "We were eating eighteen meals a day on
that thing.... By the time we got home we had our
own zip code."

And as for airplanes, she quipped, "Airlines! You
pay all that money to get aboard some type of
transportation where in the lobby they sell you a
life insurance policy."

"The worst trip I ever had was to the Bering Sea.
It was a fishing expedition that my husband talked
me into going on and he said that we could catch
salmon and we could catch Dolly Varden trout.
Now, I thought 'Dolly Varden' was a country-and-
western singer.

"I know nothing about fishing. I don't care about
fishing. So we go to the Bering Sea. We get on this
bucket that is just rolling back and forth and
rolling back and forth. I throw up in the toilet for

something like four or five days. There are flora and fauna people aboard who are really extremely weird. There's also a captain who has a palm tree...right outside of his room. And I just feel like Mr. Roberts on the USS *Reluctant,* you know?

"So I told my husband, 'You know, I hate this. I hate every part of this. No one's catching fish. No one is seeing flora, no one's seeing fauna— whomever they are—and I think what I'm going to do is I'm going to march right up to that captain and I'm going to take that palm tree and I'm going to throw it overboard. I'm going to beat on his door and say, "Captain, I've just thrown your [tree overboard]."...' And there hasn't been a day since that I haven't regretted not doing it!"

She once discussed the problem of rest rooms— an essential when you're traveling—with Joan Lunden on *Good Morning America.* "Rest rooms are very basic things when you travel. I mean, if the rest rooms are bad, I think we have to know about this. Men don't care, men do not care, no, no no, zip, zip, they're in, they're out. No, no, women have to go into a rest room. Now they've got to figure this out. I mean, what do I do in here? Do I pull a chain? Do I push something with my foot? Is there a little pedal? Do I jiggle something on the back?

Do I detonate something like a train? What do I do in this place? And until you have been in a rest room in Istanbul, I don't think you've really lived."

She vividly remembered her first trip with their children. They had bought a travel trailer that was twenty-three feet long. "We put the three kids in the back seat so that they could kick the back of the seat for five days. Then we left town for a two-week trip—just long enough for the grass to die. My husband's sitting over there reading every road map in sight. And I am behind the wheel of the station wagon, pulling the trailer along behind us. It was like dragging a nuclear-waste truck. I'm frozen to the wheel. And I must have followed Ruby and Rusty of Kendalville, Indiana, for possibly five days, because I was [too] terrified to pass them.

"And we went to see the Great Tidal Bore in New Brunswick, Canada. And this supposedly is one of these great phenomena; you know, where the water comes down the Petitcokiak River and reaches a height of eleven feet in a matter of seconds. So, you know, my husband's got the tripod out and I've got the kids in their yellow slickers and they're roped together.

"And we're standing there and we're waiting for this great rush to just suck them in. All of a sudden, it—this—this—little—*trickle* of water comes down, and it just sort of meanders and it sort of licks at your feet like, you know, a cat licking milk, or something. And I said, 'I don't believe this.' I mean, I retain more water than that. So everything has really been a disaster!"

But not all the trips were total disasters. She told *National Geographic Traveler* about a special trip the whole family took to Africa one year. "All of us went to Kenya once, but not on a tour; we traveled Ernest Hemingway-style, sleeping in tents out in the bush. We ate a lot of African dust, and we looked at the animals, which I love to do when I travel to wild places."

But, she observed, Africa had gotten crowded. "It's a lot like Times Square on New Year's Eve. And the animals know this; some of them almost seem to be posing for photographs. You expect a wildebeest to say, 'You want more leg?'"

When the children were teenagers, Erma and Bill took them on a river rafting trip. It was, in Erma's words, "The dumbest thing I have ever done in my life. You don't want to travel with teenagers, unless they're heavily sedated or you are heavily sedated, whichever comes first...

"We're standing there at the top of the south rim of the Grand Canyon and here's all this beauty around us and the one daughter, she says, 'Where's the telephone?'... One's got a comic book—eighth wonder of the world—he's reading comic books."

They once rented a house in Spain, and when Erma learned that the house came with a cook, she practically beat everyone in the family to the door: "Let's go. I'm outta here!" She explained later, "We went into town to shop for food, but in this village, near the Pyrenees, no one could speak a word of English. I don't know much Spanish, and my son, who's fluent, hadn't arrived yet. When I was buying vegetables, I'd tell them, 'My son-with-the-verbs is coming day after tomorrow. Right now, I'll just use the nouns.'" Erma's parents and her aunt also came to visit. "We had a ball," Erma recalled.

It was only natural that eventually Erma Bombeck would write a book about her travels, though she was a little hazy about where she had been. She told Larry King that she had visited at least seventy-three countries, but told Joan Lunden that same day that she and her husband Bill had been in fifty-seven countries. "Of course," she pointed out, "thirty of those countries we did in fourteen days on a

European getaway." Regardless if it was seventy-three or fifty-seven countries, it was natural that her experiences abroad would inspire a new book.

When You Look Like Your Passport Photo, It's Time to Go Home debuted in the fall of 1991. Elizabeth Crow reviewed it for the *New York Times Book Review,* noting that "Erma Bombeck writes like, sounds like and, as she admits, looks like the Arizona house-wife she is." She was not, according to Crow, "a master stylist and in truth she tends to repeat herself—is it really possible, for instance, that every tour she has ever joined has contained an identical repertory company, including one drunk, one bowel-obsessed health enthusiast and one obsessive photography nut?"

Nevertheless, what made the book work was the fact that "Erma Bombeck is always outgoing and friendly, sees people she likes everywhere and thus gives her readers a safe, cozy feeling that the world is a pretty nice place after all. This optimism holds steady, even when she's being cheated by insane drivers or being condescended to by pompous tour guides, or trying to tell a joke to a delegation of stony-faced Soviet women."

Occasionally in her travels, Erma wondered, What am I doing here? "What were we doing poking into other people's lives and cultures? Swatting their flies, worshiping at their shrines in our stocking feet, and lugging home Indonesian art to hang over our Santa Fe sofa?"

But for Erma, travel "had turned this planet into a small town—with a *Mayberry RFD* cast of people who had more in common than we had ever hoped was possible. We all had children who giggled…and a belief in something bigger than ourselves…and a need to love and be loved back. It was a start."

Holly Miller interviewed Erma in the *Saturday Evening Post,* writing, "Although some of Bombeck's travel destinations are predictable—the 21-day European getaway, the romantic Club Med cruise—she prefers obscure corners of the world. She's at her funniest on Papua, New Guinea, where she is caught in a crossfire of a tribal war, and on Easter Island, where natives refuse her cash but accept her husband's wardrobe as barter for wood carvings. She covets the anonymity of such out-of-the-way territory."

If *Passport* had a message, it was to slow down, ease up a bit, take off, and enjoy the trip. "If you want to leave your kids something special, leave them a part of the world."

Bombeck related an incident in Ireland in which she was nearly trampled by fans. "We were looking at some ruins with my parents—I love to see anything older than I am—when all of a sudden this tour bus stopped." A group from California recognized her and the bus erupted with people. "They were sweet people, but suddenly I had to suck in my stomach and smile all the time. I was public again. Maybe that's why I like places where I can really be comfortable. Let me tell you, they sure don't know me in New Guinea."

She had more negative things to say about cruises. "Cruise ships make me antsy, and I don't do beaches. My dream vacation is fast becoming a rented villa where I can relax, be part of a community, visit with the people, practice their language, and share their struggles. When I'm away from home I never think about what I do for a living. I don't take notes and I don't look for ideas. I absolutely shut down. I've heard people say they won't go on vacation without their portable phones. Who needs that? I don't want to be reminded of who I am or what I am. I prefer to blend into humanity and be a part of somebody else's life for a while."

Erma even admitted to Miller that she had outgrown writing about domestic drollery in her daily columns. But she did occasionally throw in a dust-ball joke to appease fans of her earlier years.

Maureen Conlan, books editor for the *St. Petersburg Times,* noted that Erma Bombeck might claim she was not funny in real life, but said that she *wrote* with a natural style that brimmed with humor. Erma told her that she just sat and stared into space when she composed. "Some weeks are better than others. I've had weeks like a drought."

She even tried a word processor instead of her old IBM typewriter—"but it didn't write funny," so she returned to the IBM. She told Conlan that she was not ready to retire yet, but that she did think it through "three times a week" (when her columns were due).

Kathy Hogan Trocheck quoted Erma in the *Atlanta Journal and Constitution:* "The big thing to remember about antiquity is that it is never found close to the parking lot. I don't care if it's an old monastery, a fort, a ruin, a city or an old pot, you have to walk a country mile to see it."

Asked about what she thought of the travel brochure that touted trips to exotic locales, Erma responded, "Some of the most creative fiction being written today is travel brochures. They rank right up there with Michener and Ludlum."

Bill Bombeck took his lumps in Erma's new book: "Off to the side is his food stash. These are little boxes and packets in separate bags that he clings to like diplomatic pouches that he never lets out of his sight. There's a supply of granola, crackers, dried soups, fruits, beef jerky, snacks and candy bars. I don't have the heart to tell him London is not a Third World city."

Then when he arrived at his destination, he performed an even more complicated ritual. "The moment my husband hit a hotel room, he unpacked like we had just closed an escrow for the building. Every suitcase was emptied into drawers and closets... if only for a night. Then he began his laundry. The sun could be setting over the Matterhorn. A carnival could fill the streets of Florence. The Tour de France winner could be coming over the finish line outside our hotel window. He did his laundry.

"I was also sick of lugging about his stupid tripod. A perfect stranger approached me one day in Harrods, pointed to the permanent indentation on my jumpsuit and said, 'I see you travel with a tripod.'"

CHAPTER SIXTEEN

***

A Ninth Woman

On April 23, 1992, Erma Bombeck learned that she had breast cancer. As she put it, since one out of every nine women will develop breast cancer, she had become a "ninth woman."

She would have to undergo a modified radical mastectomy of her left breast. She had faced other problems before, but none quite so personal, none quite so devastating. She couldn't help but remember all those luncheons and dinners she had attended in which they slapped a name tag on her left bosom. "Now, what shall we name the other one?" she had always asked.

But this, of course, was no laughing matter.

George Burns had always been quick to brush aside people who talked about dying: "I can't die yet. I'm booked."

Erma had a lecture to give in two weeks on the West Coast, and a commencement speech in Alabama on Mother's Day. She, too, was booked. She couldn't waste her time in the hospital.

But for once Erma was wrong. The presence of cancer was confirmed by the lab, her doctor told her, and also by an oncologist and a surgeon. Modified radical surgery would be performed the very next day to remove her breast.

Things were happening too quickly for her. But there was one thing she could do—she could be an example to her kids on how to deal with adversity. After all, she cheered people up for a living. She telephoned her son in Los Angeles and told him not to come home. She joked with her family, telling her other son not to worry until she told him to. "When will that be?" he quipped.

She and Bill forced themselves to act like everything was normal over dinner, but she couldn't keep from worrying. After dinner, she snuck into the bathroom, removed her shirt, and took a good hard look at her breasts. As she mourned the breast she would soon be losing, she became angry about how much importance society places on women's breasts, how she would be made to feel like an incomplete woman.

Her rage subsided after a few minutes, as she confronted the real problem: had the cancer spread, or was it simply in her breast?

Erma relaxed. She knew she would be able to get through the mastectomy itself. She didn't know what would happen when she came home, but she and Bill had always handled everything with a sense of humor. They would handle this the same way. But the doubts lingered.

The surgery went well. Erma's lymph nodes were clean. No metastases had occurred. She was wheeled back to her room where she waited for her surgeon.

"How are you feeling?" he questioned. Erma almost chuckled. She had a roaring headache, her body felt numb, and her throat was raw. He sat down on the bed next to her and suggested that they look at the incision together. She shook her head.

The surgeon was adamant. "I want you to look at it now. You are *not* going home to cry alone in the shower. We're going to look at this together."

He removed the bandages gently and Erma

forced herself to look at the incision. There were black stitches everywhere. She stared a long time, and then looked up as the surgeon spoke. "I want you to go home and show it to your husband."

For three days Erma stalled. Finally, she worked up enough nerve to show Bill the incision. As she carefully unwound the bandages, she found herself babbling about the stitches, and the exercises she would be taking, and all that. But what she really wanted to know was exactly what Bill was thinking. No, not thinking. *Feeling.* Was he—repulsed? In *A Marriage Made in Heaven, or, Too Tired for an Affair,* she wrote, "I searched his face carefully for his reaction. There was nothing there but love."

Erma recovered slowly, and on one visit to her surgeon she appeared surly and glum. The surgeon quickly sized up her problems. "Ah. Did all your friends stop calling and the flowers die?"

"Yes," Erma said.

He smiled and launched into a set speech crafted for just such occasions. He stressed that she was one of the lucky ones. Her cancer was small and, because it had been caught early, her lymph nodes were clean, and she would be a survivor.

As she recalled in *A Marriage Made in Heaven,* the

time for prosthesis finally came, and the surgeon handed Erma a manila envelope. He told her it wasn't a real prosthesis, but until she could be fitted, she could slip this one into her bra to be "more balanced."

As Bill drove her home, she opened the envelope and took out a small wad of cotton. "Goodness!" she cried out. "I've got bigger dust balls under my bed than this."

Erma remembered a fan who wrote, "Hey, Erma, when life gives you a bunch of lemons—stuff 'em in your bra."

Erma eventually got a fitted prosthesis—a wedge of tape that attached to her skin, with a fake breast pressed against the Velcro side doing away with the need for a bra. But it wasn't foolproof. In fact, on a plane trip shortly after the surgery, the prosthesis came loose and lodged squarely on her belly.

"Put my carry-on bag on my lap," she told Bill. "You are going to see one of the quickest bits of magic since Houdini." She put her hand into her blouse, extracted the prosthesis, and dropped it into the bag in five seconds flat.

Although her illness didn't slow Erma Bombeck down a bit, her own mortality suddenly became a pressing thought. Yes, she was beating the cancer and would hopefully be able to ward off any recurrences with proper treatment.

She had to look closely at her own development as a humorist in order to see where she was going and what the future held for her. In short, she had to take stock of her life and career.

The secret of her universal appeal, one writer said, was twofold: her relentless, studied averageness and her simple sense of humor. Indeed, studied averageness was a key phrase in describing her appeal to the general newspaper reader. But at the same time, she had created a new brand of humor—the suburban supermarket/utility room/kitchen humor of today.

"It's difficult to believe that Erma is not something entirely new in the field of American humor," Betty Dunn wrote in *Life* magazine. "Neither hayseed nor urban, never 'in,' not a black humorist, not droll or sophisticated—at her unselfconscious best, Erma's is the voice of the hearty school chum who'd let you take a spin on her bike anytime."

Herbert Mitgang regarded Erma this way: "Erma Bombeck never writes about the neutron bomb, the gross national product, Eurocommunism, the West

Bank of the Jordan…or all the tea in China. Instead, her meat-and-potatoes, fast-food themes center on her children, husband, cars, neighbors, television watching, the laundry and supermarket, her mother, honeymoons, and hair curlers. She's a cornier Doris Day, a cleaner Maude, and your Aunt Tillie on her first trip to Paris."

Erma herself observed, "About 110 percent of what I write is from real experience. All I do is watch the human condition and write it down. It's like stealing. Family vacations, for instance, provide wonderful material." Humor was always around her—in the supermarket, in the beauty parlor, and on the TV.

She had strayed somewhat from her general formula by writing *I Want to Grow Hair.* And, she moved beyond her old material in *When You Look Like Your Passport Photo,* as well. She realized that she had begun to add a new dimension to her humor: a more realistic approach to people and situations. That is, she was relying less now on wordplay and puns—she had always been a master of the pun— and more on human foibles. Her writing was becoming much more philosophical, although she hated to use that word to describe her writing talents.

She had made a breakthrough in *I Want to Grow Hair* by writing about real people, *not* fictional characters from her imagination. In *When You Look Like Your Passport Photo* she had continued in that vein, using her family openly, rather than fictionalizing them. The subject of her next book seemed obvious: she would write about her marriage.

Life magazine interviewed Erma and Bill Bombeck together to see how they usually resolved their differences: "Fights are like headaches," Erma said. "You don't plan them. But I can predict that if we're going to make a major purchase—a house, a car—we will end up shouting. Bill is so low-key he doesn't know we're arguing. He calls it 'discussing.'

"I like fights that have a life—the ones that are never resolved, the ones that you can waltz out on whenever things get dull. Our disagreement over the Persian Gulf War lasted longer than the war. I still bring it up from time to time....

"Our arguments are like monologues. I have all the lines. He's not good at it."

Bill responded, "When the Big Chill is in, I abandon all logic, cave in, and wimp out."

Erma recalled, "I did most of my complaining about how tired and overworked I was in the '50s, but ironically they were the best years of our lives—

all those babies and responsibilities, and everything was new and wondrous. The present is still challenging, but it's a sane, mellow time. We have come to terms with ourselves. I'm not going to win the Pulitzer. Bill is not going to run the Boston Marathon in under three hours. We've seen the ruins of Tikal, and we've kissed the Blarney stone. Now we drink coffee on our patio in the morning and watch birds, talk to our kids—a teacher, a writer, and a retailer—and bask in their accomplishments. We can comfort each other now as we have never done before."

Bill chimed in, "I have always liked the quote from Robert Browning: 'Grow old along with me!/ The best is yet to be.' When I first read it at twenty, it seemed sweet and sentimental. Now, at sixty-six, when I think of my wife, it's a line that makes me misty-eyed."

When asked what they would do differently if they were just getting married now, Bill answered, "I'd show up at the church with all the house paint cleaned off my ears."

Erma added, "I would be more relaxed. Marriages are basically out of your control. You're a boat in a storm. You just ride it out and hope the boat holds together. I used to think I could change things like birth, death, and struggle. You can't. You rise above them."

This passage was the most often quoted by reviewers when *A Marriage Made in Heaven, or, Too Tired for an Affair* hit the shelves in the fall of 1993:

"The impact of television on marriage was awesome," Erma wrote about her early years of marriage. "Meals were planned around it, and social life revolved around schedules.

"But mostly, television for women—especially the commercials—defined and reinforced our roles. The message was we alone bore the responsibility for the success or failure of our husbands. If we didn't feed him a rib-sticking warm breakfast, he would develop irregularities and lose clients.... And heaven forbid the boss would come to dinner and the glasses were spotted or streaked. He'd never get that promotion and it would be our fault.

"Even men began to believe it. One day Bill approached me with his shirt and sang tauntingly, 'Honey, ring around the collar.' 'So why don't you wash your crummy neck?' I snapped."

CHAPTER SEVENTEEN

❧

A Faint but Radiant Smile

Among the many letters Erma Bombeck received when she went public in 1992 with the news of her breast cancer was one from a fan named Fern Wharton Brill. Brill sympathized with Erma, offering her support to Erma for the struggles to come, if there were any.

Brill also wrote that she had waged her own fight against cancer. It seemed that at Brill's advanced age—ninety—people were much less sympathetic than they were with younger people suffering in the same way.

In fact, no one at the hospital seemed concerned about the lump Fern Brill had found in her breast.

She thought it strange that age should affect the amount of empathy she received. After an argument with the hospital, Brill finally insisted on a biopsy. Indeed, the lump did prove to be cancerous. She soon had a bilateral modified radical mastectomy.

In April 1993, Erma used Fern Brill's letter as the basis for a column, and soon the world knew what had happened to the ninety-year-old woman who thought quite correctly that she had cancer. "I think I admire this woman's pure guts and courage," Erma wrote. "She didn't roll over and do what she was told." The column was a kind of "Profile in Courage" for a woman who would not back down and keep quiet, but insisted on receiving the treatment she deserved.

A Marriage Made in Heaven, or, Too Tired for an Affair was scheduled for publication in the fall of 1993. But in July of that same year, Erma faced a far more formidable problem than promoting her new book. On July 1, she became ill, and an examination showed that her kidneys had both shut down.

"I've had polycystic kidneys all my life," she told an interviewer, explaining that it was a very slow, progressive disease. She said she had never written about this malady, although she had known she had inherited it from her father by the time she was in her twenties.

Polycystic kidney syndrome is a disease in which cysts grow on the outside of the kidneys until they cover them entirely, preventing them from performing their functions. After Erma had been thoroughly examined to make sure that there were no signs of cancer, she was released from the hospital and sent home. There, she was instructed how to administer a four-times-a-day kidney dialysis to herself.

In order to live, every six hours she would need to go into a backroom of her home in Paradise Valley to administer dialysis to herself. This dialysis treatment involved hooking herself up to an IV bag for twenty minutes, which would compensate for her failing kidneys. Keeping up courage and humor every step of the way, she hung a handmade sign above the door that read "M.A.S.H. 4091," a signal of how hospital-like her home had become.

She was adamant about taking care of herself. She was also adamant about not having her friends and family act as if these were her last days on earth. "I don't want people looking at me like I'm not gonna be here fifteen minutes later," she said. "Gimme a break! I'm doing great."

At about this time, she also went public with the fact that she had suffered two miscarriages. The reasoning behind this revelation was apparently to soften the news about her kidney failure. She had been close to personal hardship and heartbreak throughout her life. About her miscarriages, she said, "This is something you never forget. You can't put a face to the child, but you think about it forever."

Polycystic kidney disease was hereditary, and Erma was well aware that her sons had perhaps inherited it from her. Erma jokingly referred to it as "the gift that keeps on giving." She wanted to be sure she handled the disease with care. "I don't want the boys to see their mother dragging around." And so she was handling the dialysis herself while continuing to write three columns a week and finish up her eleventh book.

The good news was that she was now on a list to receive a kidney for transplant at kidney banks in both Phoenix and Los Angeles. The bad news was that it might take a year or more before such a kidney was available, since it had to be tested to find out if it matched hers.

In the meantime, she had just signed a contract with HarperCollins, her publisher, for two new books. "In the deal, negotiated with her agent Aaron Priest," *Publishers Weekly* reported, "Harper gets world and audio rights, and will publish the books in hardcover and paperback. Meanwhile, the last book in her previous three-book contract, *A Marriage Made in Heaven, or, Too Tired for an Affair,* appears next month in a first hardcover printing of 500,000 copies."

"I'm too busy to think about my condition," she told a friend. "The ideas [for the books] will come. The world changes every day and I change with it. That's all."

But there was a problem. With kidney dialysis four times a day, she was more or less a prisoner of her own house. She could not travel the country signing books and giving talks. She was pretty much hooked to that dialysis machine until her kidney transplant.

The book tour HarperCollins had arranged for *A Marriage Made in Heaven* was immediately can-celed, but Erma agreed to a series of telephone interviews. "You need a sense of humor and a good support system, otherwise you're not going to make it," she said.

When two friends in Atlanta, former Georgia First Lady Betty Talmadge and retired Rich's book buyer Faith Brunson, heard about Erma's plight, they immediately phoned to encourage her. Betty Talmadge had lost part of a leg to a blood clot in December of that year; she could certainly empathize with Erma's pain. "Erma faces hard times physically and goes right on with her life; that's what I admire," she said. "I do it, too. We have to be brave; complaining won't do any good." But humor was always Erma's top priority.

During the first days of her dialysis treatment, over thirty people—mostly fans of her column, people she did not even know—offered to donate kidneys to her. "It's really a nice thing, that people you've never met are willing to go through something like that for you. The problem is, a nonrelative donor rarely works out."

As for her converted book tour—the one by telephone—it was working out very well. Phil Donahue, *20/20,* and *Good Morning America* had all sent crews to Erma's house in Paradise Valley for interviews. Plus, newspaper reviewers telephoned from all over

the country. "This is the first time I've ever promoted a book from my house like this. I'm usually
out there on the road, hitting every whistle-stop,
every little radio station, every newspaper. Now I'm
doing it all by phone."

One reviewer came to the house directly, since
she worked for the *Arizona Republic*. Her review was
quite generous. "Bombeck occasionally takes a serious turn, as she does in her latest book," Joyce
Valdez wrote. "The book is rife with her trademark
wit (including a hilarious account of her wedding
day), but interspersed with the humor are bittersweet reflections on death, aging, a miscarriage,
and her bout with breast cancer."

She also noted, "Despite fame and fortune from
her nationally syndicated column and best-seller
books, Bombeck still dwells in the ordinary world
of bug bites, unprogrammable VCR machines and
Kmart price checks. Ask her how to reduce the
national debt, and she'll likely reply, 'How would I
know.'

"Other syndicated columnists may bluster about
the sea of red ink lapping at our shoes, but Bombeck
prefers to toss readers a lifeline of one-liners, quips,
and anecdotes."

"The thing to remember about a humor column

is, this is not a cure for cancer," joked Erma. "We're talking 500 words to get somebody's mind off Bosnia, the health plan, all that stuff. I want to get as far away from those things as I possibly can. I prefer to talk about my mother finishing her Christmas shopping.

"You read something like that and for five minutes, you don't think about the bad stuff. You think about this crazy lady who's out there wrapping her presents and gloating because it's only November and she's getting it done already!"

Joanne Kaufman gave *A Marriage Made in Heaven* a ho-hum review in *People* magazine. "If not finding Bombeck a yuk a minute is the mark of the congenitally curmudgeonly, well, so be it. This time the chronicler of domestic chaos takes on the vicissitudes of married life. When Erma Fiste married Bill Bombeck in 1949, she had big plans. She was going to turn her new husband into a new man—wrest him away from his card-playing cronies, set up schedules for him, teach him to recap ballpoint pens. Dear reader, she was doomed to failure, but she adjusted, just as Bill adjusted to her culinary clumsiness."

She continued, "If there is anything fresh to say

about class reunions, adult children who return to the nest, the difficulty of programming a VCR, the fitness boom and the sexual revolution, Bombeck fails to say it. Particularly affecting are the Bombecks' struggle to comfort each other at the untimely death of a friend and their valiant attempts to deal with Erma's breast cancer, now in remission. Unfortunately, for every truly witty or poignant passage, there is yet another gag about hot flashes and toilet flushes. All of which keeps *A Marriage Made in Heaven* from being an affair to remember."

Through all the excitement of the telephone interviews, Erma was her usual workaholic self. She was already making notes on her next book, and concentrated on turning out three columns a week.

The kidney bank didn't have good news; Erma was told she might expect a new kidney in the spring of 1994. But spring 1994 came and went, and Erma was no nearer to a transplant. The summer months were not easy for Erma that year. She was in pain and obviously suffering from her kidney failure. She was taken to the hospital, and one of her kidneys—the one most covered with cysts—was removed.

It was a complicated operation. Erma wrote her

columns several weeks ahead, writing enough items to cover the period she would spend recuperating, with the provision that her syndicate would publish columns from the past to cover the time she would spend in the hospital.

After five weeks of resting she was ready to resume writing her columns and her new book: she was back in the saddle. Her doctors also explored the possibility that her cancer might have come back—but it hadn't.

In the summer of 1995, a great deal of publicity surrounded Mickey Mantle, the Yankee baseball great, who was dying and needed a kidney transplant. He got it almost immediately. The question immediately arose in the minds of Erma's fans. Why couldn't she get a kidney any faster?

Glenna Shapiro, executive director of the Arizona Kidney Foundation, noted that Erma Bombeck's situation illustrated that prominent people did not always get preferential treatment, as Mantle was alleged to have received. She pointed out that Erma, who had been instrumental in fund-raising for the foundation, was not denied a kidney, but that no kidney had been found to match hers.

Art Buchwald knew that Erma had refused to

use her celebrity status to get moved up on the transplant waiting list. He would call her frequently during those long days when she patiently waited for that call from the foundation to come through. "She had great humor," he said later. "We would see an accident on television and we used to joke, 'Maybe that's your kidney!'"

Erma had been wearing a beeper for a number of years so that when a kidney was finally found, she would be alerted immediately. In April 1996, the beeper sounded. A kidney had been found for her. She was immediately flown to the University of California at San Francisco Medical Center, where the transplant operation was to be performed.

Friends who had been waiting for a long time for this news were cheered immeasurably by the arrival of the kidney. "It's in answer to a lot of prayers," cartoonist Bil Keane said. "Hopefully, it will be a successful transplant and she will go on to be the funny lady she's always been." He pointed out that she had weathered quite an ordeal waiting for almost five years for a proper kidney match. "She's been under such stress the last few years with the dialysis. Yet she has maintained her great optimism and sense of humor and has kept the nation laughing."

And Keane was right. Optimistic as always, Erma was awaiting the transplant more with eagerness than with fear. She knew she would be all right; that everything would work out fine in the end.

An Arizona talk-show host, Pat McMahon, said that the transplant was a tremendous relief to Bombeck's friends and fans. "She's one of those treasures that you simply can't afford to lose."

Dodie Johnes, a member of the board of the Arizona Kidney Foundation, called word of the transplant "the best news I've heard. Erma is our mentor and our fairy godmother and our inspiration."

McMahon added, "I'm waiting for the report that the hospital staff has injured itself from laughing."

The transplant, performed by Dr. William J. Amend, a transplant surgeon, on Wednesday, April 3, was a success. A hospital spokesperson—Rebecca Higbee—reported, "She's alert and talking, but not to the press."

At the same time, Erma Bombeck's eleventh book was just about to be released. It was titled *All I Know about Animal Behavior I Learned in Loehmann's Dressing Room*. She would obviously be unable to do a book tour, just as she had been unable to do one for her tenth. And yet the tenth book had done well. Why worry? But Erma wasn't there to help sell the book in the stores, and her fans missed her.

Meanwhile, things had taken a turn for the worse at the hospital. Erma's transplant surgeon said that there were complications arising from the operation. Several days after the transplant, in fact, Dr. Amend said that Erma was suffering from postoperative pneumonia. She saw the members of her family regularly, but she did not see strangers or give interviews. She was kept isolated from well-wishers.

Later, Dr. Amend had more bad news. Erma had developed jaundice from gallbladder disease. Her condition was serious. Within three weeks, it was obvious that her transplant had not taken properly. With the added complications of pneumonia and jaundice, she was seriously ailing.

On the night of April 21, all her family came in to see her and talk to her. Her daughter Betsy was there, her sons Andy and Matt, and her husband, Bill. "On that evening, she was very cheerful," said an observer. The family members finally said goodnight and slipped away quietly during the late evening hours.

It was Erma's last good-bye.

According to Dr. Amend, "Early on the morning of April 22, she died of heart failure."

An observer noted that Erma Bombeck had died with a smile on her lips. "It was a faint but radiant smile, as though she had a private joke about dying."

And indeed perhaps she did.

A Note from the Editors

This book was selected by the book division of the company that publishes *Guideposts*, a monthly magazine filled with true stories of people's adventures in faith.

Guideposts magazine is not sold on the newsstand. It is available by subscription only. And subscribing is easy. All you have to do is write to Guideposts, 39 Seminary Hill Road, Carmel, New York 10512. When you subscribe, each month you can count on receiving exciting new evidence of God's presence, His guidance and His limitless love for all of us.

Guideposts is also available on the Internet by accessing our home page on the World Wide Web at http://www.guideposts.org. Send prayer requests to our Monday morning Prayer Fellowship, read stories from recent issues of our magazines, *Guideposts, Angels on Earth, Clarity, Guideposts for Kids,* and *Positive Living,* and follow our popular book of daily devotionals, *Daily Guideposts.* Excerpts from some of our best-selling books are also available.